Prophetic PRAYERS

DAILY PRAYER GUIDE BASED ON THE BOOK OF PROVERBS

JULIO SEVERO

ISBN: 979-8-88640-115-8 (sc)
ISBN: 979-8-88640-116-5 (hc)
ISBN: 979-8-88640-117-2 (e)

Because of the dynamic nature of the Internet, any web addresses or links contained in this book may have changed since publication and may no longer be valid. The views expressed in this work are solely those of the author and do not necessarily reflect the views of the publisher, and the publisher hereby disclaims any responsibility for them.

One Galleria Blvd., Suite 1900, Metairie, LA 70001
1-888-421-2397

Julio Severo is one of those rare breed of Christian men who actually display the courage of their convictions under persecution without compromise or capitulation. His book Prophetic Prayers reflects that courage in that he lets the Bible speak for itself without watering down the message or turning it into the "fluff" that fills so many of the shelves in Christian bookstores these days. If you're looking for a prayer-resource sufficient to help you through life's toughest challenges, by someone who's actually been there, Julio's Prophetic Prayers is an excellent choice.

—Rev. Scott Lively, author of "The Pink Swastika."

Julio informs and inspires in this book. He helps the reader understand the importance of prophetic prayers. The forces of evil fear a praying man and woman. Prophetic Prayers make hell shudder!

—Rev. Michael S. Heath, Helping Hands Ministries

CONTENTS

INTRODUCTION

Prophetic times are these last days, which require prophetic vision, words, and acts. And according to 2 Timothy 3:1, the last days are also "perilous times." So a man or woman living in our time needs to be open to the Lord's supernatural presence and his special empowering anointing. What does he have in store for us in these days?

> In the last days, God says, I will pour out my Spirit on all people. Your sons and daughters will prophesy, your young men will see visions, your old men will dream dreams. Even on my servants, both men and women, I will pour out my Spirit in those days, and they will prophesy. (Acts 2:17–18)

Another translation says, "In the last days, God says, I will pour my Spirit on everyone. Your sons and daughters will *speak what God has revealed*. Your young men will see visions. Your old men will dream dreams. In those days I will pour my Spirit on my servants, on both men and women. *They will speak what God has revealed*" (GW, italics mine). The clear meaning of that promise is that in our time God will raise many men and women to declare what he has revealed. Of course, the prophetic ministry brings direction and revelations to the church, but where can you find what God has already revealed? In his Word. God wants to give this Christian generation the supernatural ability not only to proclaim the Gospel but also to declare and release prophetically his mighty Word.

Why will prophetic empowering be increased in these days? Because people who are open to God's supernatural orientation know what to do and are not easily misled.

> Where there is no revelation, the people cast off restraint.
> (Proverbs 29:18a)

Where there is prophetic direction, the people know what God wants. Therefore, *Prophetic Prayers* will give you a vision to prophesy what God wants for your life, family, city, etc.

This book brings prayers based totally on my experience in the book of Proverbs. For more than two decades, I have been using the Psalms to praise Jesus in my prayer times. Using the Psalms daily as my songbook, I learned how to have a closer relationship with my God, to know him better, and to contemplate him in my worship times. With such experience, gradually I noticed I could literally *pray Proverbs*, directing its powerful words to me and many people. I discovered in Proverbs a vast spiritual treasure of blessings, wisdom, and justice.

Proverbs is a real handbook of God's specific will for daily human behavior. While Psalms teaches you how to relate to God, Proverbs teaches you how to relate to people, and it shows you how to nurture order, decency, and good judgment *in your personal, family, and social life.* Its main subject *is not spiritual salvation but order in human relationships and behaviors.*

I wrote this guide for daily use. A typical month has thirty days, and Proverbs has 31 chapters. By reading Proverbs at the pace of the monthly calendar, you will be able to release God's blessings and righteousness daily in your life, family, church, city, and government. Therefore, each chapter of *Prophetic Prayers* has been arranged according to the date of the month corresponding to the same number of each chapter of Proverbs. Here is an example:

DAY 18

4b: the fountain of wisdom is a bubbling brook.

Suggested prayer: Lord Jesus, I open my inmost being for you, and I give full opportunities and free rein for the Lord to make your fountain of wisdom as a bubbling brook in me.

Day 18 refers to the chapter 18 of Proverbs, *4b* is verse 4 of chapter 18 of Proverbs, and *b* means that only the second part of that verse has been quoted.

When I pray in the morning, I read the chapter of Proverbs corresponding to the date of the month, I meditate in the direction of the verses, and as I feel directed by the text, I raise my right hand and release it prophetically to me and other people who need God's blessings and interventions. I only release the prophetic word in the direction I feel. It is necessary to have sensitivity to the Holy Spirit when you are reading Proverbs. He will probably give you better insights on issues I don't even address directly here.

Because my focus is prayer, I will quote only the verses that, in my view, contain an inspirational source for prayer. However, at the same time I encourage you to read in your Bible a whole chapter of Proverbs a day. Such a practice will brings us good advice so we can have excellent attitudes. Some verses lead us to prophetic prayer, and many others will teach us sensible behavior.

Of course, our spiritual knowledge is not perfect, but we have to behave in the best way we know. The apostle Paul comments in 1 Corinthians 13:9:

> For we know in part and we prophesy in part.

> We don't know everything, and our prophecies are not complete. (CEV)

> Our knowledge is incomplete and our ability to speak what God has revealed is incomplete. (GW)

He also declares that our ability "to see" spiritually is limited: "For we see now through a dim window obscurely" (1 Corinthians 13:12a, Darby). Although everything we do here on earth is imperfect, we need to act according to good judgement and with a disposition to please God.

A good piece of advice is to pray for wisdom (sees James 1:5–7), so that you may know how to live and apply the revelations of God's Word. To learn how to let the Holy Spirit guide his wisdom in you, read the appendix of this book, which addresses the life of Proverbs' author, the wisest man in the world. His life offers an excellent lesson that might help you not to waste the wisdom that comes from the Lord.

"Your Will Be Done"

When Jesus taught us to pray, "Your will be done, on earth as it is in heaven," he was showing us that our faith declaration has the power to sow that will in us and other people. God's will is what he wants to happen in the world where we live. God wants human beings to experience the reality of his will in the same way the inhabitants of the kingdom of heaven already experience it. Much of what he wants to be accomplished here on earth has been well explained in Proverbs, where we are taught the kinds of behaviors and attitudes that should become reality in our daily lives.

Proverbs inspires us to prophesy God's specific will for specific situations. It also inspires us to make creative prayers to help foster righteousness and weaken wickedness in this world. When we prophesy Proverbs for many situations, God's righteousness will break forth in individuals, moving them to know and to live God's will.

We should prophesy Proverbs the way Jesus taught us to pray. For instance, Proverbs 11:10a says, "When the righteous prosper, the city rejoices." Then, with that direction we could pray: "God, make the righteous prosper." This is not an incorrect prayer. But in the prayer Jesus taught us, he doesn't tell us to say, "Father, please make your will become reality here on earth." He taught that we should say, "Your will be done, on earth as it is in heaven." In that prayer, you are not imploring but declaring that the will of God will be done on earth. You are really prophesying the accomplishment, implementation, and execution of God's will in this world. In places where the darkness reigns, through your prophetic prayer the will of God will enter and will start to work.

Words Have Power

When God created the world, he released his words. All he needed to do was to say, "Let there be light!" And the light started to exist. God left his will written in his Word, the Bible. There are many words in the Bible about God's will for many situations and circumstances. He wants those words to be released by his children. There is power in the words that go out of our lips because God created us with such a power: "The tongue has the power of life and death" (Proverbs 18:21a).

Therefore, we should learn to use our lips responsibly. Jesus warns, "But I tell you that men will have to give account on the day of judgment for every careless word they have spoken. For by your words you will be acquitted, and by your words you will be condemned" (Matthew 12:36–37). Words have power. The best way to use that power is saying the words God says in his Word.

God wants to establish his will through our lips. He wants his will to be released through the prayers we make. We can, with the prayer Jesus taught us, declare God's will for our lives, families, city, country, etc.

The Word of God we release through our lips works as a seed (see Matthew 13:1–23). Our responsibility as spiritual farmers (see 2 Timothy 2:6) is to sow the right seed, in the right place, in the right time, and in the right people, as our knowledge allows. In the right time, that seed will produce results (see Psalm 126:5–6).

Qualified to Win

We are God's coworkers (see 1 Corinthians 3:9). In these difficult days, God wants to work with us to accomplish great victories and to establish his projects. The enemies of God want to hinder, but we will prevail: "They will fight against the Lamb; but the Lamb, *together with his called, chosen, and faithful followers*, will defeat them, because he is Lord of lords and King of kings" (Revelation 17:14 GNT, italics mine). Although the forces of darkness fight, God promises the Lamb, *and we, his faithful followers, will win with him!*

The faithful followers have been given a calling and special empowering to win.

> The LORD is pleased with his people, and he gives
> victory to those who are humble. All of you *faithful*

people, praise our glorious Lord! Celebrate and worship. Praise God with songs on your lips and *a sword in your hand.* Take revenge and punish the nations. Put chains of iron on their kings and rulers. *Punish them as they deserve*; this is the privilege of God's *faithful* people. Shout praises to the LORD! (Psalm 149:4–9 CEV, italics mine)

So the faithful followers praise God because they know they have been called to conquer victories. They have in their hands an effective sword to destroy evil. And they have authority from the Lord to carry out, as God's Word has already determined, sentences of punishment against evil forces.

In these last days in which Satan, the defeated one, increases his oppression, God wants to crown us with victory. He wants us to use the special authority he has given us to act and decide prophetically the course of families, cities, and nations through the sharp sword in our hands. That sword is the Word of God uttered by our lips under the direction of the Holy Spirit (see Hebrews 4:12 and Ephesians 6:17). We have many reasons to praise Jesus in the war against the forces of darkness, because those enlisted in Jesus's army receive training and empowering to conquer great victories even in times of oppression. "Because the LORD takes pleasure in his people. He crowns those who are oppressed with victory" (Psalm 149:4 GW). The more the oppression, the greater the honor and victory!

Kingly Authority

The authority God gives us to act prophetically is so big it is similar to the king's authority. In the past, a king had full authority to decide issues of supreme importance. When a king *said* somebody was to be arrested, freed, or promoted, *his word* was obeyed. It is such authority, spiritually speaking, that God has given us. He wants us to intervene in important issues here *on earth.* When we release, under the direction of the Spirit, God's Word for personal, family, and social changes, that Word *never* returns empty (see Isaiah 55:11).

That powerful Word is God's decree for the accomplishment and construction of all God's projects here on earth and for the destruction of all the projects of the defeated one. When we declare that Word, we are decreeing together with God—that is, we are decreeing here on earth—exactly what the King of Kings has already decreed in heaven. See what the Word of God reveals us about our right to act as kings:

> Those who receive God's overflowing kindness and the gift of his approval will *rule in life* because of one person, Jesus Christ. (Romans 5:17b GW, italics mine)

We shall reign. That is, we will use kingly authority in our lives here on earth!

> But you are a special people, a holy nation, priests and *kings,* a people given up completely to God, so that you may make clear the virtues of him who took you out of the dark into the light of heaven. (1 Peter 2:9 BBE, italics mine)

> And hath made us *kings* and priests unto God and his Father; to him *be* glory and dominion for ever and ever. Amen. (Revelation 1:6 KJV, italics mine)

> He lets us *rule as kings* and serve God his Father as priests. To him be glory and power forever and ever! Amen. (Revelation 1:6 CEV, italics mine)

> And hast made us unto our God *kings* and priests: and *we shall reign on the earth*. (Revelation 5:10 KJV, italics mine)

God has, spiritually speaking, called us to be kings here on earth. What does a king do? He rules and issues decrees. He decrees the implementation of his will in the society where he lives. God has qualified us to reign with Christ and to release through our lips the words Jesus taught: *Your will be done, on earth as it is in heaven*! So we can declare (or decree!) with faith:

> "May God's will be done in my life!"
> "May God's will be done in my family!"
> "May God's will be done in my city!"
> "May God's will be done in my country!"

In these prayers, we are giving God opportunities to activate the carrying out of his will. When we prophesy for different kinds of human situations what has already been decreed in Proverbs, the Holy Spirit gets room to trigger his specific will for those situations.

We are kings under the King of Kings and prophesy what our King has prophesied in His Word.

Warriors Who Conquer

For us to be able to conquer in battles, we should be always releasing and sowing God's Word. Even if we don't see immediate results, we need to continue prophesying. In the most difficult circumstances, we need the persistence of soldiers who do not give up.

The apostle Paul encourages us, "No, in all these things *we are more than conquerors* through him who loved us" (Romans 8:37, italics mine). *More than conquerors* is translated from the original Greek word (*hupernikao*), and it means *to be completely victorious*.

According to the Dictionary of American English published by Noah Webster in 1828, the word *conqueror* means: "One who conquers; one who gains a victory; one who subdues and brings into subjection or possession, by force or by influence. The man who defeats his antagonist in combat is a conqueror, as is the general or admiral who defeats his enemy."

As warriors, we need to use the war weapon God gives us to be successful against evil: "Take … the sword of the Spirit, which is the word of God" (Ephesians 6:17). The sword of the Spirit is the Word of God we utter. Who is qualified to release that Word to touch lives and nations? Those who are clothed with the spiritual armor. That armor is Christ's character: "Rather, clothe yourselves with the Lord Jesus Christ, and do not think about how to gratify the desires of the sinful nature" (Romans 13:14). If the armor is Christ's character, then we need that character so we can use the sword to kill and destroy the projects of the defeated one.

We should use the sword of the Spirit continually in combat, prophesying, and decreeing life to God's purposes and prophesying and decreeing death to the intentions and works of the defeated one. In these combats we can do as Moses did. When prophesying a Bible passage, we can lift our hands in prayer (see Exodus 17:10–13).

Besides, we have the responsibility to intervene and apply God's Word prophetically so the wicked may not have freedom to oppress, kill, rob, rape, and commit other kinds of wickedness. We should curse their evil actions so these actions may be weakened and destroyed. See what Psalm 141:5c teaches in several versions:

> I am always praying against their evil deeds. (GNT)

> My prayer is directed against evil deeds. (GW)

My prayer also *shall be* against their evils. (LITV)

My prayer is always against evil deeds. (WEB)

God wants us to pray against all kinds of wickedness. And he wants the authors of that wickedness to be disciplined. Of course, the wicked need salvation, as everybody else does. Our responsibility is to pray so they may come to know the Savior. But who can guarantee that most of them will want to give their lives to Jesus? And while they don't choose Jesus, can they have freedom to commit all evil they want? We cannot stop praying for God's mercy for them, but we need to understand that he gives us the authority to intervene prophetically against evil.

Just because we pray for the salvation of the wicked, does that mean they cannot be disciplined for their wickedness and crimes? Even in Christian homes, doesn't God command parents to discipline their children with the rod? Why? So the children may be trained to keep aloof from wicked attitudes, words, and ways. The purpose of the discipline is to help people turn from wrong behaviors. Therefore, Proverbs contains many passages showing that God wants the wicked to be disciplined here on earth. If we don't pray according to Proverbs, we will have to let the wicked freely commit wickedness. If we pray prophetically, they won't have freedom to continue promoting evil with carefree arrogance.

Believe!

I don't give a detailed explanation of each verse of Proverbs here, but I present principles that will help you apply prophetically many of its passages. I pray that my experience may be a springboard for you to be a source of blessings in many situations. Prophesy Proverbs believing, for Jesus said, "Everything is possible for the person who has faith" (Mark 9:23b GNT).

"Have faith in God," Jesus answered. "I tell you the truth, if anyone says to this mountain, 'Go, throw yourself into the sea,' and does not doubt in his heart but believes that what he says will happen, it will be done for him. Therefore I tell you, whatever you ask for in prayer, believe that you have received it, and it will be yours." (Mark 11:22–24)

Prophetic Prayers is especially useful for Christians who have a deeper calling for prayer and intercession. The intercessor knows how to pray for the people's salvation and knows to spend much time in that important spiritual activity.

This book does not change the intercessor's spiritual direction but just gives him or her more vision and insight so God's Word and will may be activated in a specific way in his or her life, family, and society. The intercessor with Christ's mind can use it as a very useful prayer guidebook.

Of course, the application of God's Word is something very personal in the life of each Christian. But we should do everything guided by the *fear of the Lord* that Proverbs teaches us. Before beginning each monthly day of prayer, release the following blessing on your life, based on 1 Corinthians 13:4–7.

Suggested prayer: In the name of Jesus, I prophesy, release, sow, plant, and cultivate in me a heart to love Jesus. I sow and cultivate in me a heart that is patient and kind and never gets tired of waiting. I sow and cultivate in me a heart that is not jealous or proud and will not let me think I am better than other people or behave in a haughty way. I sow and cultivate in me a heart that is not selfish, does not keep thinking about myself only, and does not try to take advantage of people. I sow and cultivate in me a heart that will help me not behave in an inappropriate, indecent, mean, and rude way. I sow and cultivate in me a heart that does not get easily angry and annoyed, does not keep sorrows and resentments, and does not keep a record of wrongs that others do. I sow and cultivate in me a heart that takes no pleasure in wrongdoing and is not happy when injustice is practiced but has always pleasure to side with truth and is glad when it prevails. I sow and cultivate in me a heart that will never give up but will persist and stay strong and loyal to Jesus in all circumstances. I sow and cultivate in me a heart full of faith, hope, and persistence. Jesus, I give full opportunities and free rein for you to make your love overflow in my heart. May your love in my heart never end.

1–4: The proverbs of Solomon son of David, king of Israel: for attaining wisdom and discipline; for understanding words of insight; for acquiring a disciplined and prudent life, doing what is right and just and fair; for giving prudence to the simple, knowledge and discretion to the young.

Get ready, in prayer, to absorb the book of Proverbs.

Suggested prayer: In the name of Jesus, I open my heart, and I let it completely open so that the Word of God of Proverbs may help me receive wisdom and discipline, understand words of insight, and live a disciplined and sensible life, doing what is right and just and fair. Allow it to give me prudence, knowledge, and good sense. I prophesy, release, sow, plant, and cultivate in my heart all the wisdom of Proverbs.

7a: The fear of the LORD is the beginning of knowledge.

Suggested prayer for you: In the name of Jesus, I prophesy, release, sow, plant, and cultivate in me the fear of the Lord. In the name of Jesus, I open my heart, and I let it completely open to the knowledge, the orientation, and the fear of the Lord in the Word of God in Proverbs. I prophesy, release, sow, plant, and cultivate in me a heart to respect, love, and obey the Lord Jesus deeply.

Suggested prayer for your children: In the name of Jesus, I prophesy, release, sow, plant, and cultivate in my sons and daughters [specify their

names] the fear of the Lord. I prophesy, release, sow, plant, and cultivate in them a heart to respect, love, and obey the Lord Jesus deeply.

Suggested prayer for other people: In the name of Jesus, I prophesy, release, sow, plant, and cultivate in [specify his or her name] the fear of the Lord. I prophesy, release, sow, plant, and cultivate in him or her a heart to respect, love, and obey the Lord Jesus deeply.

Suggested prayer for national and international authorities: In the name of Jesus, I prophesy, release, sow, plant, and cultivate [specify his or her name] the fear of the Lord. I prophesy, release, sow, plant, and cultivate in him or her a heart to respect, love, and obey the Lord Jesus deeply.

> 8–9: Listen, my son, to your father's instruction and do
> not forsake your mother's teaching. They will be a garland
> to grace your head and a chain to adorn your neck.

We can prophesy and sow obedient children.

Suggested prayer: In the name of Jesus, I prophesy, release, sow, plant, and cultivate in my sons and daughters [specify their names] a heart to listen and pay attention to the discipline and training from their father and not abandon or neglect the teachings from their mother. May this discipline, training, and teaching bring honor, excellence, and dignity in each of their lives. May the will of God be done in their lives.

6–9: For the LORD gives wisdom, and from his mouth come knowledge and understanding. He holds victory in store for the upright, he is a shield to those whose walk is blameless, for he guards the course of the just and protects the way of his faithful ones. Then you will understand what is right and just and fair—every good path.

Suggested prayer for you: In the name of Jesus, I prophesy, release, sow, plant, and cultivate in me a heart open and sensitive to God for me to seek his wisdom so that I may understand what is right, fair, and just and know what I should do.

Suggested prayer for your children: In the name of Jesus, I prophesy, release, sow, plant, and cultivate in my sons and daughters [specify their names] hearts open and sensitive to God for them to seek his wisdom so that they may understand what is right, fair, and just and know what they should do.

Suggested prayer for other people: In the name of Jesus, I prophesy, release, sow, plant, and cultivate in [specify his or her name] a heart open and sensitive to God for him or her to seek his wisdom so that he or she may understand what is right, fair, and just and know what he or she should do.

Suggested prayer for national and international authorities: In the name of Jesus, I prophesy, release, sow, plant, and cultivate in [specify his or her name] a heart open and sensitive to God for him or her to seek his wisdom so that he or she may understand what is right, fair, and just and know what he or she should do.

> 10–16: For wisdom will enter your heart, and knowledge will be pleasant to your soul. Discretion will protect you, and understanding will guard you. Wisdom will save you from the ways of wicked men, from men whose words are perverse, who leave the straight paths to walk in dark ways, who delight in doing wrong and rejoice in the perverseness of evil, whose paths are crooked and who are devious in their ways. It will save you also from the adulteress, from the wayward wife with her seductive words.

As the Lord guides you, you can prophesy verses 9 through 16.

Suggested prayer for you: In the name of Jesus, I prophesy, release, sow, plant, and cultivate in me a wise heart to love the Word of God. May Jesus's wisdom protect me and deliver me from doing evil. May Jesus's wisdom help keep me far away from people who are always telling lies. May Jesus's wisdom help me avoid immoral men or women with their seductive words.

Suggested prayer for your children: In the name of Jesus, I prophesy, release, sow, plant, and cultivate in my sons and daughters [specify their names] a wise heart to love the Word of God. May Jesus's wisdom protect them and deliver them from doing evil. May Jesus's wisdom help keep them far away from people who are always telling lies. May Jesus's wisdom help them avoid immoral men or women with their seductive words.

Suggested prayer for other people: In the name of Jesus, I prophesy, release, sow, plant, and cultivate in [specify his or her name] a wise heart to love the Word of God. May Jesus's wisdom protect and deliver him or her from doing evil. May Jesus's wisdom help keep him or her far away from people who are always telling lies. May Jesus's wisdom help him or her avoid immoral men or women with their seductive words.

> 21: For the upright will live in the land, and the blameless will remain in it.

Suggested prayer: In the name of Jesus, I prophesy, declare, and determine: may only the blameless people—of character, honesty, and integrity—be able to live and remain in my city, on TV, and in the government of my country.

> 22: But the wicked will be cut off from the land, and the unfaithful will be torn from it.

One way God "eliminates" the wicked is by leading them to a conversion experience with Jesus. When a thief, prostitute, or trafficker is transformed by Jesus, a wicked one is "eliminated." That is, an evil individual loses his or her wicked existence, and a new creature is born! Regarding the wicked who don't want to receive a transformation, just prophesy and let God take care of them. Don't worry about the results. God knows what he does.

Suggested prayer: In the name of Jesus, I prophesy, declare, and determine: may all the wicked in my city, on TV, and in the government of my country be eliminated, and may all the criminals, sorcerers, and treacherous ones be pulled by their roots and expelled from here. Lord, I deliver and put into your hands all the criminals of my city so that the Lord may act and intervene mightily to root out and sweep them from here.

DAY 3

1–2: My son, do not forget my teaching, but keep my
commands in your heart, for they will prolong your life
many years and bring you prosperity.

Suggested prayer for you: In the name of Jesus, I prophesy, release, sow, plant, and cultivate in me a heart to read, meditate, and keep the Word of God. Jesus, I open my life completely to your abundant life, prosperity, success, and peace.

Suggested prayer for your children: In the name of Jesus, I prophesy, release, sow, plant, and cultivate in my sons and daughters [specify their names] a heart to read, meditate, and keep the Word of God. Jesus, I bless them so that they may open their lives and become completely open to your abundant life, prosperity, success, and peace.

3–4: Let love and faithfulness never leave you; bind
them around your neck, write them on the tablet of
your heart. Then you will win favor and a good name
in the sight of God and man.

Suggested prayer for you: In the name of Jesus, I prophesy, release, sow, plant, and cultivate in my heart the Lord's love and faithfulness. Lord Jesus, I give you full opportunities and free rein to honor me and open up doors in my love and faithfulness to you.

Suggested prayer for your children: In the name of Jesus, I prophesy, release, sow, plant, and cultivate in the hearts of my sons and daughters [specify their names] the Lord's love and faithfulness. Lord Jesus, I bless them so that they may give you full opportunities and free rein to honor them and open up doors in their love and faithfulness to you.

Suggested prayer for other people: In the name of Jesus, I prophesy, release, sow, plant, and cultivate in the heart of [specify his or her name] the Lord's love and faithfulness. Lord Jesus, I bless him or her so that he or she may give you full opportunities and free rein to honor him or her and open up doors in his or her love and faithfulness to you.

> 5–6: Trust in the LORD with all your heart and lean not on your own understanding; in all your ways acknowledge him, and he will make your paths straight.

When following certain directions, trips, or decisions in your life, put everything before God. The ideal way is for you to remember God in *all of your commitments.*

Suggested prayer: Lord Jesus, in your name, I deliver and I put into your hands my (trip, decision, commitment, etc.), and I recognize you as my Shepherd and God who gives me victory and straightens my ways. In that situation, I give full opportunities and free rein for you to open doors, act on my behalf, guide me, show me the right way, and straighten my steps and paths.

> 7–8: Do not be wise in your own eyes; fear the LORD and shun evil. This will bring health to your body and nourishment to your bones.

Suggested prayer for you: In the name of Jesus, I prophesy, release, sow, plant, and cultivate in me a humble heart to love Jesus and avoid everything that makes the Holy Spirit sad. I open my life completely to Jesus's health.

Suggested prayer for your children: In the name of Jesus, I prophesy, release, sow, plant, and cultivate in my sons and daughters [specify their names] humble hearts to love Jesus and avoid everything that makes the Holy Spirit sad. I bless them to open their lives completely to Jesus's health.

Suggested prayer for other people: In the name of Jesus, I prophesy, release, sow, plant, and cultivate in [specify his or her name] a humble heart to love Jesus and avoid everything that makes the Holy Spirit sad. I bless him or her to open his or her life completely to Jesus's health.

> 13–15: Blessed is the man who finds wisdom, the man who gains understanding, for she is more profitable than silver and yields better returns than gold. She is more precious than rubies; nothing you desire can compare with her.

We need to cultivate an opening to the wisdom of God.

Suggested prayer for you: In the name of Jesus, I prophesy, release, sow, plant, and cultivate in me a heart open to the wisdom of God. Lord Jesus, I open my life completely to your wisdom and wise advice in the Word of God.

Suggested prayer for your children: In the name of Jesus, I prophesy, release, sow, plant, and cultivate in my sons and daughters [specify their names] hearts open to the wisdom of God. Lord Jesus, I bless them to open their lives completely to your wisdom and wise advice in the Word of God.

Suggested prayer for other people: In the name of Jesus, I prophesy, release, sow, plant, and cultivate in [specify his or her name] a heart open to the wisdom of God. Lord Jesus, I bless him or her to open his or her life completely to your wisdom and wise advice in the Word of God.

More precious than a ruby is also a wife of noble character (see Proverbs 31:10). A wise wife is a man's best counselor. If you are married, sow such a woman in your wife:

Suggested prayer: In the name of Jesus, I prophesy, release, sow, plant, and cultivate in my wife a wise heart to help me with wise and prudent advice. Lord Jesus, I open my life completely to the wise advice of my wife.

If you are single, go along investing and sowing:

Suggested prayer: In the name of Jesus, I prophesy, release, sow, plant, and cultivate in my future wife a wise heart to help me with wise and prudent advice. Lord Jesus, I open my life completely to the wise advice of my future wife.

> 21: My son, preserve sound judgment and discernment,
> do not let them out of your sight.

Suggested prayer for you: In the name of Jesus, I prophesy, release, sow, plant, and cultivate in me the good sense, discretion, and prudence of Jesus.

Suggested prayer for your children: In the name of Jesus, I prophesy, release, sow, plant, and cultivate in my sons and daughters [specify their names] the good sense, discretion, and prudence of Jesus.

Suggested prayer for other people: In the name of Jesus, I prophesy, release, sow, plant, and cultivate in [specify his or her name] the good sense, discretion, and prudence of Jesus.

> 23–26: Then you will go on your way in safety, and
> your foot will not stumble; when you lie down, you
> will not be afraid; when you lie down, your sleep will

be sweet. Have no fear of sudden disaster or of the ruin that overtakes the wicked, for the LORD will be your confidence and will keep your foot from being snared.

If you have really allowed Jesus's good sense and prudence guide your life, then prophesy with faith.

Suggested prayer: In the name of Jesus, I prophesy and declare: may Jesus's good sense and prudence help me follow, without tripping, my way in safety. May Jesus's wisdom give me calm sleep and protect me from all fear and concern whenever I lie down. May Jesus's foresight protect me from fears, dangers, sudden calamities, and the ruin and destruction that reach the wicked. Lord Jesus, I declare you are my Protector, God, who keeps me from being snared. I take refuge in you.

33b: he blesses the home of the righteous.

If you already have Jesus's righteousness in your life, then declare with faith:

Suggested prayer: Lord Jesus, I open my home completely to all your blessings, success, and prosperity. Lord Jesus, I give you full opportunities and free rein to do special visitations in my home and bless it.

34a: He mocks proud mockers.

To understand that text better, read the comment of verse 35b.

Suggested prayer: Lord Jesus, I give you full opportunities and free rein to mock all the sorcerers and proud mockers in my city, on TV, and in the government of my country who mock everything the Lord approves and respect everything the Lord does not approve.

35a: The wise inherit honor.

Suggested prayer for you: In the name of Jesus, I prophesy, sow, plant, and cultivate in me a wise heart to inherit glory, honor, and prestige.

Suggested prayer for your children: In the name of Jesus, I prophesy, sow, plant, and cultivate in my sons and daughters [specify their names] wise hearts to inherit glory, honor, and prestige.

Suggested prayer for other people: In the name of Jesus, I prophesy, sow, plant, and cultivate in [specify his or her name] a wise heart to inherit glory, honor, and prestige.

35b: fools he holds up to shame.

Are you sad to see individuals on TV, and in other places committing and defending, shamelessly, what is evil in the eyes of God? Do you think there is not anything you can do to stop immorality and antifamily values? On the contrary, you have in your hands and in your lips the most powerful tool in the universe: the authority of the Word of God. When you see the wicked doing evil on TV, for example, point your arms to them and prophesy: "In the name of Jesus, I prophesy that those fools will suffer more and more shame in their wickedness." If you just hear about what they are doing without seeing them, then lift your hands and declare that same prayer. If you are in the presence of fools committing unacceptable acts before God, then repeat the below prayer audibly. Seek a place away from other people and prophesy or prophesy quietly in your spirit. Be discreet.

Remember also to prophesy their conversion. If they repent and accept Jesus, everything will go right for them. If they decide to remain in their wickedness, they will suffer more and more shame. The result will be very obvious: someone who suffers shame in committing wickedness will want to stop committing wickedness. That is a prayer to discourage them from evil. Just because a wicked person doesn't want to change his or her lifestyle doesn't mean he or she should have total freedom to practice all the kinds of evil that he or she wants.

> Even though you are kind to the wicked, they never learn to do what is right. Even here in a land of righteous people they still do wrong; they refuse to recognize your greatness. Your enemies do not know that you will punish them. LORD, put them to shame and let them suffer; let them suffer the punishment you have prepared. Show them how much you love your people. (Isaiah 26:10–11 GNT)

We cannot force the wicked to repent and accept Jesus, but we can prophesy against all their wickedness against other people. It is our responsibility to intervene prophetically. Remember: whenever the fools suffer shame for their foolishness and perversions, they will want to change their lifestyles or at least abandon their perverted behavior.

Suggested prayer: In the name of Jesus, I prophesy and declare: may shame, dishonor, and humiliation be the only promotion and reward that all the fools and sorcerers in my city, on TV, and in the government of my country will receive for their immoral and perverted acts and words. Lord, I give you full opportunities and free rein to embarrass and hold up to shame these shameless individuals who despise what is right in your eyes. May God's will be done in their situation.

DAY 4

8–9: Esteem [wisdom], and she will exalt you; embrace her, and she will honor you. She will set a garland of grace on your head and present you with a crown of splendor.

Since Proverbs is a book where the wisdom of God is manifested and since God wants us to obtain that wisdom, it is our responsibility to read and absorb that book daily, with much prayer and our hearts open to the Holy Spirit. In the right time, the harvest for your life will be honor from God before other people.

Suggested prayer for you: In the name of Jesus, I prophesy, sow, plant, and cultivate in me a heart to love, welcome, value, and live the wisdom of the Word of God. Lord Jesus, I give full opportunities and free rein for the wisdom of your Word to raise me up, bring me great honors and promotions, and give me a beautiful and glorious crown of grace and happiness.

Suggested prayer for your children: In the name of Jesus, I prophesy, sow, plant, and cultivate in my sons and daughters [specify their names] a heart to love, welcome, value, and live the wisdom of the Word of God. Lord Jesus, I bless them to give full opportunities and free rein for the wisdom of your Word to raise them up, bring them great honors and promotions, and give them a beautiful and glorious crown of grace and happiness.

Suggested prayer for other people: In the name of Jesus, I prophesy, sow, plant, and cultivate in [specify his or her name] a heart to love, welcome, value and live the wisdom of the Word of God. Lord Jesus, I bless him to give full opportunities and free rein for the wisdom of your Word to raise him up, bring him great honors and promotions, and give him a beautiful and glorious crown of grace and happiness.

> 18: The path of the righteous is like the first gleam of dawn, shining ever brighter till the full light of day.

When following a direction in your life, put everything before God. The ideal way is for you to remember God in *all of your commitments.*

Suggested prayer for you: Lord Jesus, in your name, I deliver and put into your hands my life course, and I give you full opportunities and free rein to show me the right way and guide me with your shining light in my way and in everything I do.

Suggested prayer for your children: Lord Jesus, in your name, I deliver and put into your hands the life course of my sons and daughters [specify their names], and I bless them to give you full opportunities and free rein to show them the right way and guide them with your shining light in their way and in everything they do.

Suggested prayer for other people: Lord Jesus, in your name, I deliver and put into your hands the life course of [specify his or her name], and I bless him or her to give you full opportunities and free rein to show him the right way and guide him with your shining light in his or her way and in everything he or she does.

1–2: My son, pay attention to my wisdom, listen well to my words of insight, that you may maintain discretion and your lips may preserve knowledge.

It is interesting that Septuagint adds this advice at the end of that last verse: "Give no heed to a worthless woman" (Brenton). It is a perfect contrast: while a woman who leads a life of love and obedience to God is "worth far more than rubies," a woman who lives for the carnal pleasures is "a worthless woman." Since the following verses warn about the immoral woman's danger, the message here is especially useful for men, single and married. Man, prophesy to your own life!

Suggested prayer for you: In the name of Jesus, I prophesy, sow, plant, and cultivate in me a heart attentive to the wisdom and ears open to accept, welcome, and practice the words of good sense and good advice, so that I may know how to behave with good sense, discretion, prudence, and intelligence and so I don't pay any attention to worthless women.

Suggested prayer for your children: In the name of Jesus, I prophesy, sow, plant, and cultivate in my sons and daughters [specify their names] a heart attentive to the wisdom and ears open to accept, welcome, and practice the words of good sense and good advice, so that they may know how to behave with good sense, discretion, prudence, and intelligence and so they don't pay any attention to worthless women.

8: Keep to a path far from her, do not go near the door
of her house.

Suggested prayer for you: Lord Jesus, I deliver and give into your hands my life, so that the Lord may act and intervene mightily in my situation, so that I may keep far away from worthless women and so that I may never go near their houses.

Suggested prayer for you: In the name of Jesus, I prophesy, sow, plant, and cultivate in me a heart open to accept, welcome, and practice good advice and to walk in the right way, far away from worthless women.

Suggested prayer for your children: Lord Jesus, I deliver and give into your hands my sons [specify their names], so that the Lord may act and intervene mightily in their situation, so that they may keep far away from worthless women, and so that they may never go near their houses.

Suggested prayer for your children: In the name of Jesus, I prophesy, sow, plant, and cultivate in my sons [specify their names] hearts open to accept, welcome, and practice good advice and to walk in the right way, far away from worthless women.

Suggested prayer for other people: Lord Jesus, I deliver and give into your hands [add his name], so that the Lord may act and intervene mightily in his situation, so that he may keep far away from worthless women and so that he may never go near their houses.

Suggested prayer for other people: In the name of Jesus, I prophesy, sow, plant, and cultivate in [add his name] a heart open to accept, welcome, and practice good advice and to walk in the right way, far away from worthless women.

15–18: Drink water from your own cistern, running
water from your own well. Should your springs overflow

in the streets, your streams of water in the public squares? Let them be yours alone, never to be shared with strangers. May your fountain be blessed, and may you rejoice in the wife of your youth.

Husband, your wife is a fountain of life. Bless her!

Suggested prayer: In the name of Jesus, I prophesy, sow, plant, and cultivate my wife as a fountain of life for the Lord. In the name of Jesus, I prophesy, sow, plant, and cultivate in my wife the richest spiritual, emotional, physical, and material blessings.

Another version says: "Be faithful to your own wife and give your love to her alone. So be happy with your wife and find your joy with the woman you married" (Proverbs 5:15,18 GNT).

Suggested prayer: In the name of Jesus, I prophesy, sow, plant, and cultivate in me a heart to be faithful to my wife and to give my love only to her. I prophesy, sow, plant, and cultivate in me a heart to have joy and always be happy with the woman I married (or with the woman I am going to marry).

> 19: A loving doe, a graceful deer—may her breasts satisfy you always, may you ever be captivated by her love.

Husband, bless your wife.

Suggested prayer: In the name of Jesus, I prophesy, sow, plant, and cultivate my wife as a loving gazelle and a graceful and gentle doe. May her breasts satisfy me abundantly in every time, and may her love always make me happy. Lord Jesus, I give you full opportunities to keep me always attracted and captivated by the love of my wife.

12–15: A scoundrel and villain, who goes about with a corrupt mouth, who winks with his eye, signals with his feet and motions with his fingers, who plots evil with deceit in his heart—he always stirs up dissension. Therefore disaster will overtake him in an instant; he will suddenly be destroyed—without remedy.

You don't need to know the Word of God to understand that it is wrong to lie, rob, and support perversions like witchcraft, adultery, homosexuality, abortion, etc. There are people who are not Christian and are correctly aware of those problems. Of course, the perverts need transformation by Jesus. But while they do not repent, should they have free rein to harm innocent people? Should they face no hindrances?

Suggested prayer: In the name of Jesus, I prophesy and declare: may disgrace, ruin, disaster, and calamity befall all the acts and words of all the sorcerers and perverts in my city, on TV, and in the government of my country. May they be completely brought down and fall in shame for their wickedness. May they be completely broken, and may they in this brokenness have opportunities to look for and experience Jesus's transforming grace. May they have opportunities to know Jesus and be raised up to do his will. May the will of God be done in their lives.

16–19: There are six things the LORD hates, seven that are detestable to him: haughty eyes, a lying tongue, hands that shed innocent blood, a heart that devises wicked schemes, feet that are quick to rush into evil, a false witness who pours out lies and a man who stirs up dissension among brothers.

God hates and is disgusted by the six kinds of bad character described here.

The lying tongues are detestable to him, although in our time all lies from the media are loved. He hates hearts that devise perverse plans. Some years ago, I attended a meeting where the government's leaders were devising plans to establish social conditions, with the help of the media, so that adolescents could receive a sexual education free from moral limits, where they might learn how to enjoy sex without worrying about marriage, morality, etc. God detests plans like these. Of course, he doesn't want to kill the individuals involved in that wickedness. But he doesn't want them to have a free rein in their perverted actions. All that he hates deserves to be weakened. For instance, does an abortion doctor whose hands have shed innocent blood deserve to prosper financially and enjoy a life full of material comfort? Absolutely not.

Suggested prayer: In the name of Jesus, I prophesy and declare: may the haughty eyes, the lying tongues, the hands that shed innocent blood, the hearts that devise perverse plans, the feet that are quick to rush into evil, the false witnesses who spread lies, and the individuals who provoke discord among brothers be completely weakened and embarrassed in their wickedness. In the name of Jesus, I prophesy and declare: may all the individuals involved in that wickedness in my city, on TV, and in the government of my country suffer shame more and more in their evil actions. May the will of God be done in those situations.

> 20–24: My son, keep your father's commands and do not forsake your mother's teaching. Bind them upon your heart forever; fasten them around your neck.

When you walk, they will guide you; when you sleep, they will watch over you; when you awake, they will speak to you. For these commands are a lamp, this teaching is a light, and the corrections of discipline are the way to life, keeping you from the immoral woman, from the smooth tongue of the wayward wife.

If you have small children, now it is the time to sow in them! Place your hand on their heads and prophesy.

Suggested prayer: In the name of Jesus, I prophesy, sow, plant, and cultivate in my sons and daughters [specify their names] hearts open to the teachings of the Word of God. I prophesy, sow, plant, and cultivate in them a heart fertile to the seed of the Word of God. I prophesy and declare that when they walk and lead their lives, the Word of God will guide them and will give them direction, with assistance from the Holy Spirit. When they sleep, the Lord will protect them. When they awake, the Holy Spirit will speak to them through the Word. May the Word of God bring light to their lives, lead them to good ways, and protect them from immoral women and their flattering words.

5: [wisdom and understanding] will keep you from the adulteress, from the wayward wife with her seductive words.

Men, the Word of God always advises you concerning immoral women's danger and their seductive words. Cultivate this advice in your heart.

Suggested prayer for you: In the name of Jesus, I prophesy, sow, plant, and cultivate in me a wise and intelligent heart obedient to the Word of God to keep me far away from the beautiful fool women and their seductive words.

Suggested prayer for your children: In the name of Jesus, I prophesy, sow, plant, and cultivate in my sons [specify their names] wise and intelligent hearts obedient to the Word of God to keep them far away from the beautiful fool women and their seductive words.

Suggested prayer for other people: In the name of Jesus, I prophesy, sow, plant, and cultivate in [specify his name] a wise and intelligent heart obedient to the Word of God to keep him far away from the beautiful fool women and their seductive words.

13–14: She took hold of him and kissed him and with a brazen face she said: "I have fellowship offerings at home; today I fulfilled my vows."

It is not difficult to come across immoral women in the world. But the passage refers to a woman who, at least in the religious appearance, was not an unbeliever. She was a *believer*! Then the obvious warning is that dangerous sexual temptations are not confined to *unbelieving* women.

Suggested prayer for you: In the name of Jesus, I prophesy, sow, plant, and cultivate in me a wise heart to keep me far away from the beautiful fool women and their seductive words, even if they are *believers*. In the name of Jesus, I won't let my heart think about a woman like that, and neither will I try to come near her.

Suggested prayer for your children: In the name of Jesus, I prophesy, sow, plant, and cultivate in my sons [specify their names] wise hearts to keep them far away from the beautiful fool women and their seductive words, even if they are *believers*. In the name of Jesus, I bless them not let their hearts think about a woman like that or try to come near her.

Suggested prayer for other people: In the name of Jesus, I prophesy, sow, plant, and cultivate in [specify his name] a wise heart to keep him far away from the beautiful fool women and their seductive words, even if they are *believers*. In the name of Jesus, I bless him for him not let his heart think about a woman like that or try to come near her.

Wives, mothers, and sisters, help the men in your life. Prophesy on them!

Suggested prayer: In the name of Jesus, I prophesy, sow, plant, and cultivate in the heart of [specify his name] wisdom and understanding from the Word of God. I prophesy and declare: may wisdom and good sense help him keep far away from the beautiful fool women and their seductive words, even if they are *believers*. In the name of Jesus, may his heart not let him think about a woman like that or let him try to come near her.

8: All the words of my mouth are just; none of them is crooked or perverse.

The whole chapter 8 of Proverbs exalts the qualities of wisdom. Let us sow such wisdom in our lives.

Suggested prayer for you: In the name of Jesus, I prophesy, sow, plant, and cultivate in me the wisdom of God and lips to say important, noble, and excellent words and speak what is right and defend truth and justice. I prophesy, sow, plant, and cultivate in me a heart and lips that will not say twisted, lying, deceiving, and false words.

Suggested prayer for your children: In the name of Jesus, I prophesy, sow, plant, and cultivate in my sons and daughters [specify their names] the wisdom of God and lips to say important, noble, and excellent words and speak what is right and defend truth and justice. I prophesy, sow, plant, and cultivate in them hearts and lips that will not say twisted, lying, deceiving, and false words.

Suggested prayer for other people: In the name of Jesus, I prophesy, sow, plant, and cultivate in [specify his or her name] the wisdom of God and lips to say important, noble, and excellent words and speak what is right and defend truth and justice. I prophesy, sow, plant, and cultivate in him a heart and lips that will not say twisted, lying, deceiving, and false words.

11: for wisdom is more precious than rubies, and nothing you desire can compare with her.

Suggested prayer for you: In the name of Jesus, I prophesy, sow, plant, and cultivate in me a wisdom more precious than rubies.

Suggested prayer for your children: In the name of Jesus, I prophesy, sow, plant, and cultivate in my sons and daughters [specify their names] a wisdom more precious than rubies.

Suggested prayer for other people: In the name of Jesus, I prophesy, sow, plant, and cultivate in [specify his or her name] a wisdom more precious than rubies.

12: I, wisdom, dwell together with prudence; I possess knowledge and discretion.

Suggested prayer for you: In the name of Jesus, I prophesy, sow, plant, and cultivate in me a heart to have pleasure in prudence, knowledge, and good sense.

Suggested prayer for your children: In the name of Jesus, I prophesy, sow, plant, and cultivate in my sons and daughters [specify their names] hearts to have pleasure in prudence, knowledge, and good sense.

Suggested prayer for other people: In the name of Jesus, I prophesy, sow, plant, and cultivate in [specify his or her name] a heart to have pleasure in prudence, knowledge, and good sense.

13: To fear the LORD is to hate evil; I hate pride and arrogance, evil behavior and perverse speech.

Suggested prayer for you: In the name of Jesus, I prophesy, sow, plant, and cultivate in me a heart to fear the Lord and hate evil, pride, immodesty, bad behavior, and perverse and false words.

Suggested prayer for your children: In the name of Jesus, I prophesy, sow, plant, and cultivate in my sons and daughters [specify their names] hearts to fear the Lord and hate evil, pride, immodesty, bad behavior, and perverse and false words.

Suggested prayer for other people: In the name of Jesus, I prophesy, sow, plant, and cultivate in [specify his or her name] a heart to fear the Lord and hate evil, pride, immodesty, bad behavior, and perverse and false words.

> 14: Counsel and sound judgment are mine; I have understanding and power.

Suggested prayer for you: Lord Jesus, I open my life completely so that your wisdom may give me wise advice, understanding, prudence, and strength.

Suggested prayer for your children: Lord Jesus, I bless my sons and daughters [specify their names] to open their lives completely so that your wisdom may give them wise advice, understanding, prudence, and strength.

Suggested prayer for other people: Lord Jesus, I bless [specify his or her name] to open his or her life completely so that your wisdom may give him or her wise advice, understanding, prudence, and strength.

> 15–16: By me kings reign and rulers make laws that are just; by me princes govern, and all nobles who rule on earth.

This is addressed to men who work in the government and have high positions.

Suggested prayer for you: In the name of Jesus, I prophesy, sow, plant, and cultivate in me an open heart to let the wisdom of God help me govern and make good laws. Lord Jesus, I give full opportunities and free rein for your wisdom to guide me in my high position.

Suggested prayer for other people: In the name of Jesus, I prophesy, sow, plant, and cultivate in [specify his or her name] an open heart to let the wisdom of God help him or her govern and make good laws. Lord Jesus, I bless him or her to give full opportunities and free rein for your wisdom to guide him or her in his or her high position.

> 17: I love those who love me, and those who seek me
> find me.

Suggested prayer for you: In the name of Jesus, I prophesy, sow, plant, and cultivate in me a heart to love the wisdom of God.

Suggested prayer for your children: In the name of Jesus, I prophesy, sow, plant, and cultivate in my sons and daughters [specify their names] hearts to love the wisdom of God.

Suggested prayer for other people: In the name of Jesus, I prophesy, sow, plant, and cultivate in [specify his or her name] a heart to love the wisdom of God.

> 18–19: With me are riches and honor, enduring wealth
> and prosperity. My fruit is better than fine gold; what I
> yield surpasses choice silver.

Suggested prayer: In the name of Jesus, I open my life completely to the wisdom of God and its wealth, honor, prosperity, and justice and fruits, which are better than fine gold.

20–21: I walk in the way of righteousness, along the paths of justice, bestowing wealth on those who love me and making their treasuries full.

Suggested prayer: In the name of Jesus, I prophesy, sow, plant, and cultivate in me an open heart to love the wisdom of God. I open my life completely for the wisdom of God to guide me to walk in ways and paths of justice, directing me always to do what is right and grant me wealth and fill my treasures.

33–34: Listen to my instruction and be wise; do not ignore it. Blessed is the man who listens to me, watching daily at my doors, waiting at my doorway.

Suggested prayer for you: In the name of Jesus, I open my life completely to hear attentively the instructions of the wisdom of God. In the name of Jesus, I prophesy, sow, plant, and cultivate in me an open heart to remain daily very attentive to what the wisdom of God is going to tell me.

Suggested prayer for your children: In the name of Jesus, I bless my sons and daughters [specify their names] to open their lives completely to hear attentively the instructions of the wisdom of God. In the name of Jesus, I prophesy, sow, plant, and cultivate in them open hearts to remain daily very attentive to what the wisdom of God is going to tell them.

Suggested prayer for other people: In the name of Jesus, I bless [specify his or her name] to open his or her life completely to hear attentively the instructions of the wisdom of God. In the name of Jesus, I prophesy, sow, plant, and cultivate in him or her an open heart to remain daily very attentive to what the wisdom of God is going to tell him or her.

10–11: The fear of the LORD is the beginning of wisdom, and knowledge of the Holy One is understanding. For through me your days will be many, and years will be added to your life.

The obvious meaning of this passage is that the people who live according to the wisdom of the Word of God may have added years of life to use their wisdom to bless their families, churches, and cities. So let us prophesy what God wants! Besides, we really have to bless all the wise people of God regularly, because they need our prayers: "And pray in the Spirit on all occasions with all kinds of prayers and requests. With this in mind, be alert and *always keep on praying for all the saints*" (Ephesians 6:18, italics mine). You can also specify that prayer for all the wise Christians you know.

Suggested prayer: In the name of Jesus, I prophesy, release, sow, plant, and cultivate in the whole people of God in my city fear of the Lord, wisdom, and knowledge of the Holy One. I prophesy, release, sow, plant, and cultivate the multiplication of the years of the wise people of God who have been using their wisdom for Christ's cause. I bless them so they may live many blessed and victorious years using their wisdom to advance Kingdom of God here on earth.

DAY 10

1: A wise son brings joy to his father, but a foolish son grief to his mother.

See what the Word of God shows. If a son is not wise and does not make his father happy, even his mother eventually experiences unhappiness. If you are a father, pray this way:

Suggested prayer for your children: In the name of Jesus, I prophesy, release, sow, plant, and cultivate in my sons and daughters [specify their names] wise hearts to make me happy.

Suggested prayer if you are a child: In the name of Jesus, I prophesy, release, sow, plant, and cultivate in me a wise heart to make my father happy.

2b: righteousness delivers from death.

Suggested prayer for you: Lord Jesus, I prophesy, release, sow, plant, and cultivate your righteousness in my life, so that your righteousness may deliver me from death and failure.

Suggested prayer for you: Lord Jesus, I deliver and place my project [specify it] into your hands, so that your righteousness may deliver it from death and failure.

Suggested prayer for you: Lord Jesus, I prophesy, release, sow, plant, and cultivate your righteousness in my project [specify it], so that your righteousness may deliver it from death and failure.

Suggested prayer for your children: Lord Jesus, I prophesy, release, sow, plant, and cultivate your righteousness in my sons and daughters [specify their names], so that your righteousness may deliver them from death and failure.

Suggested prayer for other people: Lord Jesus, I prophesy, release, sow, plant, and cultivate your righteousness in [specify his or her name], so that your righteousness may deliver him or her from death and failure.

3a: The LORD does not let the righteous go hungry.

Are you going through some difficult situation? Prophesy.

Suggested prayer: Lord Jesus, in the situation I am going through, I give you full opportunities and free rein for you to supply me abundantly.

4b: diligent hands bring wealth.

Suggested prayer for you: In the name of Jesus, I prophesy, release, sow, plant, and cultivate in me diligent hands to bring me wealth. In the name of Jesus, I bless, prophesy, and declare that my diligent hands will bring me wealth.

Suggested prayer for your children: In the name of Jesus, I prophesy, release, sow, plant, and cultivate in my sons and daughters [specify their names] diligent hands to bring them wealth. In the name of Jesus, I bless, prophesy, and declare that their diligent hands will bring them wealth.

Suggested prayer for other people: In the name of Jesus, I prophesy, release, sow, plant, and cultivate in [specify his or her name] diligent hands to bring him or her wealth. In the name of Jesus, I bless, prophesy and declare that his or her diligent hands will bring him or her wealth.

6a: Blessings crown the head of the righteous.

Are you a Christian who has been living according to Lord Jesus's will? Know that he has special blessings for you!

Suggested prayer for you: I open my life completely so that the precious and special blessings from the Lord will come to crown my head.

Suggested prayer for children who lead righteous lives: I bless my sons and daughters [specify their names] to open their lives completely so that the precious and special blessings from the Lord will come to crown their heads.

Suggested prayer for other people who live righteous lives: I bless [specify his or her name] to open his or her life completely so that the precious and special blessings from the Lord will come to crown his or her head.

11a: The mouth of the righteous is a fountain of life.

Suggested prayer for you: In the name of Jesus, I prophesy, sow, plant, and cultivate in me a mouth that is a fountain of life.

Suggested prayer for your children: In the name of Jesus, I prophesy, sow, plant, and cultivate in my sons and daughters [specify their names] a mouth that is a fountain of life.

Suggested prayer for other people: In the name of Jesus, I prophesy, sow, plant, and cultivate in [specify his or her name] a mouth that is a fountain of life.

12b: love covers over all wrongs.

Suggested prayer for you: In the name of Jesus, I prophesy, sow, plant, and cultivate in me Jesus's love that covers all wrongs.

Suggested prayer for your children: In the name of Jesus, I prophesy, sow, plant, and cultivate in my sons and daughters [specify their names] Jesus's love that covers all wrongs.

Suggested prayer for other people: In the name of Jesus, I prophesy, sow, plant, and cultivate in [specify his or her name] Jesus's love that covers all wrongs.

13b: a rod is for the back of him who lacks judgment.

The rod is to control the excesses of those who lack judgement. God knows that the rod is a necessary tool of discipline. Therefore, we need to release that powerful word, especially when we see senseless people shamelessly defending wickedness, adultery, homosexuality, abortion, etc., and still receiving praises on TV.

Suggested prayer: In the name of Jesus, I prophesy and declare: may all fools with perverse and twisted hearts and minds in my city, on TV, and in the government of my country receive discipline and correction, not praises. I prophesy, declare, and release the rod, discipline, and correction to the backs of those senseless individuals, so that their conduct may be controlled and not harm anyone. May the chastening will of God be done in them.

14a: Wise men store up knowledge.

God wants us to have discretion and humility about the wisdom he gives us. In his ministry on earth, Jesus was the wisest man in the world, but he walked only with humble people, without glorying. He didn't try to show everyone how big his wisdom was.

Suggested prayer for you: In the name of Jesus, I prophesy, sow, plant, and cultivate in me a discreet and humble heart, for me to store up all the knowledge I can and only use it in humility.

Suggested prayer for your children: In the name of Jesus, I prophesy, sow, plant, and cultivate in my sons and daughters [specify their names] discreet and humble hearts, for them to store up all the knowledge they can and only use it in humility.

Suggested prayer for other people: In the name of Jesus, I prophesy, sow, plant, and cultivate in [specify his or her name] a discreet and humble heart, for him or her to store up all the knowledge he or she can and only use it in humility.

17a: He who heeds discipline shows the way to life.

Suggested prayer for you: In the name of Jesus, I prophesy, sow, plant, and cultivate in me a heart to welcome, accept, and pay attention to instruction, correction, discipline, and criticism.

Suggested prayer for your children: In the name of Jesus, I prophesy, sow, plant, and cultivate in my sons and daughters [specify their names] hearts to welcome, accept, and pay attention to instruction, correction, discipline, and criticism.

Suggested prayer for other people: In the name of Jesus, I prophesy, sow, plant, and cultivate in [specify his or her name] a heart to welcome, accept, and pay attention to instruction, correction, discipline, and criticism.

19b: he who holds his tongue is wise.

Suggested prayer for you: In the name of Jesus, I prophesy, sow, plant, and cultivate in me a wise, sensible, and prudent heart to control my own tongue and keep my lips closed when necessary.

Suggested prayer for your children: In the name of Jesus, I prophesy, sow, plant, and cultivate in my sons and daughters [specify their names] wise, sensible, and prudent hearts to control their own tongues and keep their lips closed when necessary.

Suggested prayer for other people: In the name of Jesus, I prophesy, sow, plant, and cultivate in [specify his or her name] a wise, sensible, and prudent heart to control his or her own tongue and keep his or her lips closed when necessary.

20a: The tongue of the righteous is choice silver.

Suggested prayer for you: In the name of Jesus, I prophesy, sow, plant, and cultivate in me a righteous heart and a precious tongue that is like pure silver.

Suggested prayer for your children: In the name of Jesus, I prophesy, sow, plant, and cultivate in my sons and daughters [specify their names] righteous hearts and precious tongues that are like pure silver.

Suggested prayer for other people: In the name of Jesus, I prophesy, sow, plant, and cultivate in [specify his or her name] a righteous heart and a precious tongue hat is like pure silver.

21a: The lips of the righteous nourish many.

Suggested prayer for you: In the name of Jesus, I prophesy, sow, plant, and cultivate in me righteous lips to say words that will spiritually nourish many people.

Suggested prayer for your children: In the name of Jesus, I prophesy, sow, plant, and cultivate in my sons and daughters [specify their names] righteous lips to say words that will spiritually nourish many people.

Suggested prayer for other people: In the name of Jesus, I prophesy, sow, plant, and cultivate in [specify his or her name] righteous lips to say words that will spiritually nourish many people.

22: The blessing of the LORD brings wealth, and he adds no trouble to it.

Suggested prayer for you: I open my life completely to the blessings of the Lord, which bring wealth and prosperity without adding any suffering.

Suggested prayer for your children: I bless my sons and daughters [specify their names] to open their lives completely to the blessings of the Lord, which bring wealth and prosperity without adding any suffering.

Suggested prayer for other people: I bless [specify his or her name] to open his or her life completely to the blessings of the Lord, which bring wealth and prosperity without adding any suffering.

24b: what the righteous desire will be granted.

Suggested prayer: Lord Jesus, I open my life completely for you to visit me and grant the desires I have been presenting in your presence.

27a: The fear of the LORD adds length to life.

Suggested prayer for you: In the name of Jesus, I prophesy, sow, plant, and cultivate in me passion for Jesus and the fear of the Lord, which prolongs life.

Suggested prayer for your children: In the name of Jesus, I prophesy, sow, plant, and cultivate in my sons and daughters [specify their names] passion for Jesus and the fear of the Lord, which prolongs life.

Suggested prayer for other people: In the name of Jesus, I prophesy, sow, plant, and cultivate in [specify his or her name] passion for Jesus and the fear of the Lord, which prolongs life.

28a: The prospect of the righteous is joy.

Suggested prayer: Lord Jesus, in my expectations before you, I open my life completely to the happiness and surprises of the Lord for me.

29a: The way of the LORD is a refuge for the righteous.

Suggested prayer for you: In the name of Jesus, I prophesy, sow, plant, and cultivate in me a righteous heart to walk only in the way of the Lord for me and let him be my fortress and protection.

Suggested prayer for your children: In the name of Jesus, I prophesy, sow, plant, and cultivate in my sons and daughters [specify their names] righteous hearts to walk only in the way of the Lord for them and let him be their fortress and protection.

Suggested prayer for other people: In the name of Jesus, I prophesy, sow, plant, and cultivate in [specify his or her name] a righteous heart to walk only in the way of the Lord for him or her and let him be his or her fortress and protection.

30a: The righteous will never be uprooted.

Suggested prayer: Lord Jesus, I declare you my Rock, and I prophesy that I won't be moved, I won't fail, but I will have safety.

31a: The mouth of the righteous brings forth wisdom.

Suggested prayer for you: In the name of Jesus, I prophesy, sow, plant, and cultivate in me a mouth to speak words of wisdom and prudence.

Suggested prayer for your children: In the name of Jesus, I prophesy, sow, plant, and cultivate in my sons and daughters [specify their names] mouths to speak words of wisdom and prudence.

Suggested prayer for other people: In the name of Jesus, I prophesy, sow, plant, and cultivate in [specify his or her name] a mouth to speak words of wisdom and prudence.

31b: a perverse tongue will be cut out.

If you hear individuals on TV, the radio, or other places praising perversion, prophesy! Of course their perverse tongues will be cut out in a spiritual sense, not real.

Suggested prayer: In the name of Jesus, I prophesy and declare: may the mouth of all the liars and perverted in my city, on TV, and in the government of my country be silenced, and may their perverted tongues be cut out. I bless them so that when they give up their lives to Jesus they will receive pure and righteous tongues.

4b: righteousness delivers from death.

Another version says: "righteousness saves from death" (GW). Are some of your projects in danger of failing? Prophesy.

Suggested prayer for you: Lord Jesus, I prophesy, release, sow, plant, and cultivate your righteousness in my life, so that your righteousness may deliver me from death and failure. May the will of God be done in that situation.

Suggested prayer for you: Lord Jesus, I deliver and place my project [specify it] into your hands, so that your righteousness may deliver it from death and failure. May the will of God be done in that situation.

Suggested prayer for you: Lord Jesus, I prophesy, release, sow, plant, and cultivate your righteousness in my project [specify it], so that your righteousness may deliver it from death and failure. May the will of God be done in that situation.

Suggested prayer for your children: Lord Jesus, I prophesy, release, sow, plant, and cultivate your righteousness in my sons and daughters [specify their names], so that your righteousness may deliver them from death and failure. May the will of God be done in that situation.

Suggested prayer for other people: Lord Jesus, I prophesy, release, sow, plant, and cultivate your righteousness in [specify his or her name], so that your righteousness may deliver him from death and failure. May the will of God be done in that situation.

> 5a: The righteousness of the blameless makes a straight way for them.

Suggested prayer: Lord Jesus, I give you full opportunities and free rein for your righteousness in me to guide, open, and prosper my way.

> 5b: the wicked are brought down by their own wickedness.

Suggested prayer: In the name of Jesus, I prophesy and declare: may all the wicked and sorcerers in my city, on TV, and in the government of my country be brought down by their wickedness. May they have opportunities to know Jesus and be raised up to do his will. May the will of God be done in their situations.

> 6a: The righteousness of the upright delivers them.

Is some cause or problem in your life seemly impossible to solve? If you have been living an upright life before God, then prophesy.

Suggested prayer: Lord Jesus, I give you full opportunities and free rein for your righteousness in me to deliver, protect, and rescue me.

> 8a: The righteous man is rescued from trouble.

Are you suffering anguish? Open the door of your life to Jesus's visitation.

Suggested prayer: Lord Jesus, I open my life completely for you to visit me and deliver, protect, and rescue me from every anguish and tribulation.

10a: When the righteous prosper, the city rejoices.

When the people who are righteous before God prosper, the city where they live rejoices and also prospers. So let us bless those people!

Suggested prayer: In the name of Jesus, I prophesy, release, sow, plant, and cultivate the success and the prosperity of God in all the righteous people in my city, on TV, and in the government of my country. May the will of God be done in those people.

11a: Through the blessing of the upright a city is exalted.

When the people who are righteous before God bless the city where they live, it experiences growth, prosperity, and the honor of God. So let us cultivate the habit of blessing the city where we live!

Suggested prayer: In the name of Jesus, I bless [add the name of your city]. I prophesy, release and sow the blessings of the Lord in [add the name of your city]. May the will of God be done in my city.

12: A man who lacks judgment derides his neighbor, but
a man of understanding holds his tongue.

Suggested prayer for you: In the name of Jesus, I prophesy, release, sow, plant, and cultivate in me a wise and prudent heart to control my tongue and keep quiet without ridiculing people.

Suggested prayer for your children: In the name of Jesus, I prophesy, release, sow, plant, and cultivate in my sons and daughters [specify their names] wise and prudent hearts to control their tongues and keep quiet without ridiculing people.

Suggested prayer for other people: In the name of Jesus, I prophesy, release, sow, plant, and cultivate in [specify his or her name] a wise and prudent heart to control his or her tongue and keep quiet without ridiculing people.

14: For lack of guidance a nation falls, but many advisers make victory sure.

You can bless and help change the direction of your country!

Suggested prayer: In the name of Jesus, I prophesy, release, sow, plant, and cultivate many prudent, wise, and righteous advisers in the government of my country, state, and city.

16a: A kindhearted woman gains respect.

You can prophesy that blessing to your wife, daughter, sister, etc. God wants us to bless women.

Suggested prayer: In the name of Jesus, I prophesy, release, sow, plant, and cultivate in [add her name] a kind and gracious heart to gain and conquer respect, honor, and glory.

18b: he who sows righteousness reaps a sure reward.

Have you been sowing righteousness on earth? God has sure rewards for you!

Suggested prayer for you: Lord Jesus, I open my life completely to your rewards.

Suggested prayer for you: In the name of Jesus, I prophesy, release, sow, plant, and cultivate in me a heart to sow righteousness.

Suggested prayer for your children: In the name of Jesus, I prophesy, release, sow, plant, and cultivate in my sons and daughters [specify their names] hearts to sow righteousness.

Suggested prayer for other people: In the name of Jesus, I prophesy, release, sow, plant, and cultivate in [specify his or her name] a heart to sow righteousness.

20a: The LORD detests men of perverse heart.

Suggested prayer: Lord Jesus, I give you full opportunities and free rein to block the wicked ways of all the sorcerers and other individuals of perverse heart in my city, on TV, and in the government of my country, who plan and use their words and attitudes to promote what God hates. May they be completely detained in their wickedness, in the name of Jesus. May they have opportunities to know Jesus and be raised up to do his will.

21a: Be sure of this: The wicked will not go unpunished.

Do you see the wicked killing, raping, and robbing with no authority able to hinder them? Prophesy!

Suggested prayer: In the name of Jesus, I prophesy and declare: may all the wicked and sorcerers in my city, on TV, and in the government of my country not go unpunished. I deliver and place them into the just hands of God. May the will of God be done in their situation.

23a: The desire of the righteous ends only in good.

Righteous people's desires have a happy end.

Suggested prayer: Lord Jesus, I deliver and I place into your hands the desires of my heart [specify them], so that the Lord may act and intervene mightily in those situations. I give full opportunities and free rein for you to fulfill them in my life. May the will of God be done in my life.

25: A generous man will prosper; he who refreshes others will himself be refreshed.

Are you generous and always blessing other people? Then take advantage of this promise!

Suggested prayer: Lord Jesus, I open my life completely to your rewards, blessings, and prosperity.

Suggested prayer for other generous people: Lord Jesus, I bless [specify his or her name] to open his or her life completely to your rewards, blessings, and prosperity.

28b: the righteous will thrive like a green leaf.

Suggested prayer for you: Lord Jesus, I give you full opportunities and free rein for you to prosper me and make me bloom as a healthy plant.

Suggested prayer for your children: Lord Jesus, I prophesy, release, sow, plant, and cultivate in my sons and daughters [specify their names] your righteousness, and I bless them to give you full opportunities and free rein to prosper them and make them bloom as a healthy plant.

Suggested prayer for other people: Lord Jesus, I prophesy, release, sow, plant, and cultivate in [specify his or her name] your righteousness, and I bless him to give you full opportunities and free rein to prosper him and make him bloom as a healthy plant.

29b: the fool will be servant to the wise.

Suggested prayer: In the name of Jesus, I prophesy and declare: may all the fools in my city, on TV, and in the government of my country be servants of the wise.

30a: The fruit of the righteous is a tree of life.

Have you been doing some work and investment for Jesus's sake? Consecrate every work that you do with that prayer.

Suggested prayer: In the name of Jesus, I prophesy, release, sow, plant, cultivate, and consecrate my work as a tree of life.

31: If the righteous receive their due on earth, how much more the ungodly and the sinner!

Do you see the wicked shamelessly defending wickedness, adultery, homosexuality, abortion, etc.? Prophesy!

Suggested prayer: In the name of Jesus, I prophesy and declare: may all the wicked and sorcerers in my city, on TV, and in the government of my country receive right here on earth the punishments they deserve, so that they feel the need to look for God and abandon evil. I deliver and place them into the just hands of God. May the will of God be done in their situations.

1a: Whoever loves discipline loves knowledge.

Suggested prayer for you: In the name of Jesus, I prophesy, release, sow, plant, and cultivate in me a heart to love discipline, instruction, correction, and training.

Suggested prayer for your children: In the name of Jesus, I prophesy, release, sow, plant, and cultivate in my sons and daughters [specify their names] hearts to love discipline, instruction, correction, and training.

2a: A good man obtains favor from the LORD.

If you have really led a lifestyle that is pleasing to the Lord, then let him give you blessings today.

Suggested prayer: Lord Jesus, I open my life completely to receive your favors.

2b: the LORD condemns a crafty man.

Suggested prayer: Lord Jesus, I give you full opportunities and free rein to condemn and discipline all the individuals in my city, on TV, and in the government of my country who plan wickedness (for instance, to introduce sodomy or abortion laws, etc.).

3a: A man cannot be established through wickedness.

Do you see the wicked shamelessly defending wickedness, adultery, homosexuality, abortion, etc.? Prophesy! It is not the will of God that the wicked may be established and have prosperity in a foundation of wickedness.

Suggested prayer: In the name of Jesus, I prophesy and declare: may all the wicked and sorcerers in my city, on TV, and in the government of my country not be established and prosper in their wickedness.

4a: A wife of noble character is her husband's crown.

If you are married, then sow that kind of woman *in your wife!*

Suggested prayer: In the name of Jesus, I prophesy, release, sow, plant, and cultivate a noble, virtuous, diligent, and strong character in my wife. I prophesy her as my crown, pride, and joy.

Even as a single man, you can sow a wife of noble character in your life.

Suggested prayer: In the name of Jesus, I prophesy, release, sow, plant, and cultivate in my life a virtuous and diligent wife with a strong character who will be my crown, pride, and joy.

Suggested prayer for your daughters: In the name of Jesus, I prophesy, release, sow, plant, and cultivate in my daughters [specify their names] a noble, virtuous, diligent and strong character. I prophesy that she will be the crown, pride, and joy of her husband.

5a: The plans of the righteous are just.

Suggested prayer: Lord Jesus, I open my mind, thoughts, and plans completely to your righteousness. I prophesy, release, sow, plant, and cultivate in them your righteousness.

6b: the speech of the upright rescues them.

Suggested prayer for you: In the name of Jesus, I prophesy, release, sow, plant, and cultivate in all the righteous people in my city, on TV, and in the government of my country mouths to release prophetic words of deliverance, words that will bring into existence supernatural rescue and help to the innocent people.

Suggested prayer for your children: In the name of Jesus, I prophesy, release, sow, plant, and cultivate your righteousness in my sons and daughters [specify their names], and I bless their mouths to release prophetic words of deliverance, words that will bring into existence supernatural rescue and help to the innocent people.

Suggested prayer for other people: In the name of Jesus, I prophesy, release, sow, plant, and cultivate your righteousness in [specify his or her name], and I bless his or her mouth to release prophetic words of deliverance, words that will bring into existence supernatural rescue and help to the innocent people.

7a: Wicked men are overthrown and are no more.

Do you see the wicked shamelessly defending wickedness, adultery, homosexuality, abortion, etc.? Prophesy! It is not the will of God for them to remain standing in their wickedness.

Suggested prayer: In the name of Jesus, I prophesy and declare: may all the wicked, criminals, and sorcerers in my city, on TV, and in the government of my country be overthrown and disappear. May they have opportunities to know Jesus and be raised up to do his will. May the will of God be done in these situations.

8b: men with warped minds are despised.

Do you see the wicked shamelessly defending wickedness, adultery, homosexuality, abortion, etc., and still receiving praises on TV? Prophesy!

Suggested prayer: In the name of Jesus, I prophesy and declare: may all the wicked with foolish and perverted hearts and minds in my city, on TV, and in the government of my country be despised, not praised. May they have opportunities to know Jesus and be raised up to do his will. May the will of God be done in these situations.

12b: the root of the righteous flourishes.

Suggested prayer: Lord Jesus, I give you full opportunities and free rein to give me deep roots in you, which will make me bloom and produce many fruits in you.

14a: From the fruit of his lips a man is filled with good things.

Suggested prayer for you: In the name of Jesus, I prophesy, release, sow, plant, and cultivate in me a mouth to speak the Word of God and the words of the Holy Spirit.

Suggested prayer for your children: In the name of Jesus, I prophesy, release, sow, plant, and cultivate in my sons and daughters [specify their names] mouths to speak the Word of God and the words of the Holy Spirit.

Suggested prayer for other people: In the name of Jesus, I prophesy, release, sow, plant, and cultivate in [specify his or her name] a mouth to speak the Word of God and the words of the Holy Spirit.

15b: a wise man listens to advice.

Suggested prayer for you: In the name of Jesus, I prophesy, release, sow, plant, and cultivate in me a wise heart to hear good advice.

Suggested prayer for your children: In the name of Jesus, I prophesy, release, sow, plant, and cultivate in my sons and daughters [specify their names] wise hearts to hear good advice.

Suggested prayer for other people: In the name of Jesus, I prophesy, release, sow, plant, and cultivate in [specify his or her name] a wise heart to hear good advice.

16b: a prudent man overlooks an insult.

Suggested prayer for you: In the name of Jesus, I prophesy, release, sow, plant, and cultivate in me a prudent heart to pay no attention to insults.

Suggested prayer for your children: In the name of Jesus, I prophesy, release, sow, plant, and cultivate in my sons and daughters [specify their names] prudent hearts to pay no attention to insults.

Suggested prayer for other people: In the name of Jesus, I prophesy, release, sow, plant, and cultivate in [specify his or her name] a prudent heart to pay no attention to insults.

18b: the tongue of the wise brings healing.

Suggested prayer for you: In the name of Jesus, I prophesy, release, sow, plant, and cultivate in me a wise heart with a tongue to bring healing.

Suggested prayer for your children: In the name of Jesus, I prophesy, release, sow, plant, and cultivate in my sons and daughters [specify their names] wise hearts with tongues to bring healing.

Suggested prayer for other people: In the name of Jesus, I prophesy, release, sow, plant, and cultivate in [specify his or her name] a wise heart with a tongue to bring healing.

19a: Truthful lips endure forever.

Suggested prayer for you: In the name of Jesus, I prophesy, release, sow, plant, and cultivate in me truthful lips that always will tell the truth.

Suggested prayer for your children: In the name of Jesus, I prophesy, release, sow, plant, and cultivate in my sons and daughters [specify their names] truthful lips that always will tell the truth.

Suggested prayer for other people: In the name of Jesus, I prophesy, release, sow, plant, and cultivate in [specify his or her name] truthful lips that always will tell the truth.

21a: No harm befalls the righteous.

We have no power to do anything, but we speak what the Word speaks!

Suggested prayer: In the name of Jesus, as a righteous man [or woman] in Jesus Christ, I prophesy and declare: may no harm and injustice hit me. By the authority of the Word of God, I forbid all harm from hitting me.

21b: the wicked have their fill of trouble.

Suggested prayer: In the name of Jesus, I prophesy and declare: may all the wicked and sorcerers in my city, on TV, and in the government of my country be so overwhelmed by problems and troubles that they will have no time to promote homosexuality, abortion, and other perversions. May they suffer all the consequences of their wickedness, as the Lord has already determined in his Word. May they have opportunities to know Jesus and be raised up to do his will. May the will of God be done in their situation.

22a: The LORD detests lying lips.

It is not only you, but the Lord also hates when lying words on TV, the radio, or other places praise perversion! Let us prophesy change!

Suggested prayer: In the name of Jesus, I prophesy and declare: may the mouth of all the liars in my city, on TV, and in the government of my country be silenced and detained.

23a: A prudent man keeps his knowledge to himself.

Suggested prayer: In the name of Jesus, I prophesy, release, sow, plant, and cultivate in me a prudent, modest, and humble heart to help me not to be boastful of my own knowledge but to keep me in silence and not let me say everything I know.

24a: Diligent hands will rule.

Do you work with all dedication, attention, and honesty?

Suggested prayer: In the name of Jesus, I prophesy and declare: may my diligent hands rule and conquer positions of power and authority. I prophesy that with my diligent hands I will be a leader.

You can also sow those blessed hands for you: Just look at your hands and prophesy on them!

Suggested prayer: In the name of Jesus, I prophesy, release, sow, plant, and cultivate in me diligent hands to rule.

26a: A righteous man is cautious in friendship.

Suggested prayer for you: In the name of Jesus, I prophesy, release, sow, plant, and cultivate in me an honest heart, to be cautious in friendships.

Suggested prayer for your children: In the name of Jesus, I prophesy, release, sow, plant, and cultivate in my sons and daughters [specify their names] honest hearts, to be cautious in friendships.

Suggested prayer for other people: In the name of Jesus, I prophesy, release, sow, plant, and cultivate in [specify his or her name] an honest heart, to be cautious in friendships.

1a: A wise son heeds his father's instruction.

Suggested prayer for fathers, for their children: In the name of Jesus, I prophesy, release, sow, plant, and cultivate in my sons and daughters [specify their names] wise hearts to welcome and love my instruction, correction, teaching, and discipline.

2a: From the fruit of his lips a man enjoys good things.

Suggested prayer for you: In the name of Jesus, I prophesy, release, sow, plant, and cultivate in me a mouth to speak righteous words to help people grow spiritually.

Suggested prayer for your children: In the name of Jesus, I prophesy, release, sow, plant, and cultivate in my sons and daughters [specify their names] mouths to speak righteous words to help people grow spiritually.

Suggested prayer for other people: In the name of Jesus, I prophesy, release, sow, plant, and cultivate in [specify his or her name] a mouth to speak righteous words to help people grow spiritually.

3a: He who guards his lips guards his life.

Suggested prayer for you: In the name of Jesus, I prophesy, release, sow, plant, and cultivate in me a wise, sensible, and prudent heart to keep and control my mouth and do not let me speak too much.

Suggested prayer for your children: In the name of Jesus, I prophesy, release, sow, plant, and cultivate in my sons and daughters [specify their names] wise, sensible, and prudent hearts to keep and control their mouths and do not let them speak too much.

Suggested prayer for other people: In the name of Jesus, I prophesy, release, sow, plant, and cultivate in [specify his or her name] a wise, sensible and prudent heart to keep and control his or her mouth and do not let him or her speak too much.

4b: the desires of the diligent are fully satisfied.

Are you a Christian who fulfills his responsibilities diligently before God and people? Then open yourself up for God to fulfill your desires.

Suggested prayer: Lord Jesus, I give you full opportunities and free rein for you to satisfy my desires thoroughly. I prophesy and declare that my diligent work will reward me with more than enough.

5a: The righteous hate what is false.

Do you or another person have a problem with lies or fibs?

Suggested prayer for you: In the name of Jesus, I prophesy, release, sow, plant, and cultivate in me a righteous heart to detest falsehood and hate to tell lies.

Suggested prayer for other people: In the name of Jesus, I prophesy, release, sow, plant, and cultivate in [specify his or her name] a righteous heart to detest falsehood and hate to tell lies.

5b: the wicked bring shame and disgrace.

Suggested prayer: In the name of Jesus, I prophesy and declare: may all the sorcerers and wicked in my city, on TV, and in the government of my country who promote evil with lies and falsehood be completely demoralized and embarrassed. May they have opportunities to know Jesus and be raised up to do his will.

6a: Righteousness guards the man of integrity.

Another version says: "Righteousness protects the honest way of life" (GW). In your projects, prophesy and release the righteousness of God.

Suggested prayer: Lord Jesus, in my integrity before you, I give you full opportunities and free rein to use your righteousness to protect and keep me safe.

6b: wickedness overthrows the sinner.

Suggested prayer: In the name of Jesus, I prophesy and declare: may all wickedness bring down completely from their evil stand all the sorcerers and criminals in my city, on TV, and in the government of my country, so that they may know that sin doesn't pay. May they have opportunities to know Jesus and be raised up to do his will. May the will of God be done in their situation.

7: One man … pretends to be poor, yet has great wealth.

Suggested prayer: In the name of Jesus, I prophesy, release, sow, plant, and cultivate in me a humble heart with modest words and attitudes.

9a: The light of the righteous shines brightly.

Suggested prayer for you: Lord Jesus, I give you full opportunities and free rein to make your Word in my life and my witness for you to shine brightly.

Suggested prayer for other people: Lord Jesus, I give you full opportunities and free rein to make your Word in [specify his or her name]'s life and his or her witness for you to shine brightly.

9b: the lamp of the wicked is snuffed out.

Suggested prayer: In the name of Jesus, I prophesy and declare: may all the sorcerers and wicked in my city, on TV, and in the government of my country lose all direction and light in their wicked ways.

10b: wisdom is found in those who take advice.

To ask or accept advice from prudent and wise people is an opportunity to gain wisdom.

Suggested prayer for you: In the name of Jesus, I prophesy, release, sow, plant, and cultivate in me a heart to accept and welcome good advice from wise people.

Suggested prayer for your children: In the name of Jesus, I prophesy, release, sow, plant, and cultivate in my sons and daughters [specify their names] hearts to accept and welcome good advice from wise people.

Suggested prayer for other people: In the name of Jesus, I prophesy, release, sow, plant, and cultivate in [specify his or her name] a heart to accept and welcome good advice from wise people.

12b: a longing fulfilled is a tree of life.

Suggested prayer for you: Lord Jesus, I give you full opportunities and free rein to satisfy the longings of my heart. May my fulfilled longings be as a tree of life, bringing many blessings, in the name of Jesus.

Suggested prayer for your children: Lord Jesus, I bless my sons and daughters [specify their names] to give you full opportunities and free rein to satisfy the longings of their hearts. May their fulfilled longings be as a tree of life, bringing many blessings, in the name of Jesus.

Suggested prayer for other people: Lord Jesus, I bless [specify his or her name] to give you full opportunities and free rein to satisfy the longings of his or her heart. May his or her fulfilled longings be as a tree of life, bringing many blessings, in the name of Jesus.

13a: He who scorns instruction will pay for it.

Have you already seen people defending sin using the Bible, just as the gay activists do who say that homosexuality is not sin? Prophesy.

Suggested prayer: In the name of Jesus, I prophesy and declare: may all the mockers, gay activists, and sorcerers in my city, on TV, and in the government of my country suffer all the consequences of their contempt for the values from the Word of God. May they have opportunities to know Jesus and be raised up to do his will.

13b: he who respects a command is rewarded.

Do you obey the commandments of God? Then know that he has rewards, peace, and safety.

Suggested prayer for you: Lord Jesus, I open my life completely to your rewards, blessings, peace, safety, and prosperity. May the will of God be done in my life.

14: The teaching of the wise is a fountain of life, turning a man from the snares of death.

If you have already received the wisdom that comes from God, then prophesy.

Suggested prayer: In the name of Jesus, I prophesy, release, sow, plant, and cultivate in the people my teachings and instructions as a fountain of life, to turn them from the snares of death.

15a: Good understanding wins favor.

Suggested prayer for you: Lord Jesus, I prophesy, release, sow, plant, and cultivate in me your discretion, good sense, and good understanding. I give you full opportunities and free rein to use my discretion, good sense, and good understanding for me to gain the people's approval. May they be touched by my good witness.

Suggested prayer for your children: Lord Jesus, I prophesy, release, sow, plant, and cultivate in my sons and daughters [specify their names] your discretion, good sense, and good understanding. I bless them to give you full opportunities and free rein to use their discretion, good sense, and good understanding for them to gain the people's approval. May they be touched by their good witness.

Suggested prayer for other people: Lord Jesus, I prophesy, release, sow, plant, and cultivate in [specify his or her name] your discretion, good sense, and good understanding. I bless him or her to give you full opportunities and free rein to use his or her discretion, good sense, and good understanding for him or her to gain the people's approval. May they be touched by his or her good witness.

16a: Every prudent man acts out of knowledge.

Suggested prayer for you: In the name of Jesus, I prophesy, release, sow, plant, and cultivate in me a prudent and intelligent heart to know how to use knowledge and good sense, act in that knowledge and good sense, and always think well before acting.

Suggested prayer for your children: In the name of Jesus, I prophesy, release, sow, plant, and cultivate in my sons and daughters [specify their names] prudent and intelligent hearts to know how to use knowledge and good sense, act in that knowledge and good sense, and always think well before acting.

Suggested prayer for other people: In the name of Jesus, I prophesy, release, sow, plant, and cultivate in [specify his or her name] a prudent and intelligent heart to know how to use knowledge and good sense, act in that knowledge and good sense, and always think well before acting.

> 18a: He who ignores discipline comes to poverty and shame.

Those who despise discipline need to feel that there are consequences for their disrespectful attitudes.

Suggested prayer: In the name of Jesus, I prophesy and declare: may everyone in my city, on TV, and in the government of my country who reject the correction and discipline of the Lord be overwhelmed by shame, and may they experience poverty, so that they may feel need to look for God. May they have opportunities to know Jesus and be raised up to do his will.

> 18b: whoever heeds correction is honored.

This word can be applied to children and any other person. But it is also useful for us. Is there someone who never needs a correction and a life-giving rebuke? God has honor for those who welcome discipline.

Suggested prayer for you: In the name of Jesus, I prophesy, release, sow, plant, and cultivate in me a heart to welcome the reprehension, the correction, the discipline, and the life-giving rebuke.

Suggested prayer for your children: In the name of Jesus, I prophesy, release, sow, plant, and cultivate in my sons and daughters [specify their names] hearts to welcome the reprehension, the correction, the discipline, and the life-giving rebuke.

Suggested prayer for other people: In the name of Jesus, I prophesy, release, sow, plant, and cultivate in [specify his or her name] a heart to welcome the reprehension, the correction, the discipline, and the life-giving rebuke.

19a: A longing fulfilled is sweet to the soul.

Suggested prayer: Lord Jesus, I open my life completely for you to accomplish and fulfill the longings of my heart.

20a: He who walks with the wise grows wise. Good (or bad) friendships have a very big influence.

Suggested prayer for you: In the name of Jesus, I prophesy, release, sow, plant, and cultivate in me a heart to walk only with wise people.

Suggested prayer for your children: In the name of Jesus, I prophesy, release, sow, plant, and cultivate in my sons and daughters [specify their names] hearts to walk only with wise people.

Suggested prayer for other people: In the name of Jesus, I prophesy, release, sow, plant, and cultivate in [specify his or her name] a heart to walk only with wise people.

21a: Misfortune pursues the sinner.

Suggested prayer: In the name of Jesus, I prophesy and declare: may failure pursue all the efforts of individuals in my city, on TV, and in the government of my country who want to promote or legalize abortion, homosexuality, and other perversions. May they have opportunities to know Jesus and be raised up to do his will.

21b: prosperity is the reward of the righteous.

If God promises prosperity for the righteous, who are we to retort or reject it?

Suggested prayer for you: Lord Jesus, I open my life completely to your rewards, blessings, and prosperity.

Suggested prayer for other people: In the name of Jesus, I prophesy, release, sow, plant, and cultivate rewards, blessings, and prosperity in all the righteous people in my city, on TV, and in the government of my country.

22a: A good man leaves an inheritance for his children's children.

Suggested prayer: In the name of Jesus, I prophesy, release, sow, plant, and cultivate in me a good heart that will leave an inheritance of the Lord for my children's children.

22b: a sinner's wealth is stored up for the righteous.

It is the will of God that wicked people's wealth will be kept for the righteous. Who are we to despise the will of God? Understand that the Lord is completely just in his will. If the wicked repent and open their hearts for Jesus to transform them, they will become righteous and their wealth will be stored up for themselves. If not, they will not deserve any wealth. The result is obvious: having no riches, they will feel the need to seek God!

Suggested prayer: In the name of Jesus, I prophesy, declare, and determine: may the wealth of all the sorcerers, wicked, and perverts in my city, on TV, and in the government of my country be kept and transferred to the hands of the righteous. May the will of God be done in those situations.

> 24: He who spares the rod hates his son, but he who
> loves him is careful to discipline him.

Say this prayer even if you are not married yet. God wants you to use the rod of discipline to bless your children's lives before they develop undesirable and harmful habits. You can also apply that prayer to other couples who need that blessing.

Suggested prayer: In the name of Jesus, I prophesy, release, sow, plant, and cultivate in me a heart to love my children and discipline them as soon as possible with all care and without any hesitation and delay. I prophesy, release, sow, plant, and cultivate in me a wise heart to never fail to use the rod when necessary but to apply it whenever an act of disobedience, stubbornness, and challenge may require it.

DAY 14

1a: The wise woman builds her house.

If you are married, then bless your wife. Sow that kind of wise woman in her!

Suggested prayer: In the name of Jesus, I prophesy, release, sow, plant, and cultivate in my wife a wise-wife heart to build, establish, and strengthen our family.

Even as a single person, you can sow a wise wife in your life.

Suggested prayer: In the name of Jesus, I prophesy, release, sow, plant, and cultivate in my life a wise wife to build, establish, and strengthen our family.

Suggested prayer for your daughters: In the name of Jesus, I prophesy, release, sow, plant, and cultivate in my daughters a wise-wife heart to build, establish, and strengthen their families.

Suggested prayer for your sisters: In the name of Jesus, I prophesy, release, sow, plant, and cultivate in my sisters a wise-wife heart to build, establish, and strengthen their families.

3a: A fool's talk brings a rod to his back.

Do you see fools shamelessly bragging of sins like adultery, homosexuality, abortion, etc.? Prophesy!

Suggested prayer: In the name of Jesus, I prophesy and declare: may all the fools in my city, on TV, and in the government of my country be punished, with rod in their backs, for their arrogant and foolish words. I deliver and place them into the just hands of God.

5a: A truthful witness does not deceive.

Suggested prayer: In the name of Jesus, I prophesy, release, sow, plant, and cultivate on TV and in all the courts in my city sincere witnesses who will not deceive but will tell the whole truth.

6b: knowledge comes easily to the discerning.

Suggested prayer for you: In the name of Jesus, I prophesy, release, sow, plant, and cultivate in me an intelligent mind and heart that is able to get knowledge easily.

Suggested prayer for your children: In the name of Jesus, I prophesy, release, sow, plant, and cultivate in my sons and daughters [specify their names] intelligent minds and hearts that are able to get knowledge easily.

Suggested prayer for other people: In the name of Jesus, I prophesy, release, sow, plant, and cultivate in [specify his or her name] an intelligent mind and heart that is able to get knowledge easily.

8a: The wisdom of the prudent is to give thought to their ways.

Wisdom helps us make appropriate decisions in our undertakings and plans.

Suggested prayer for you: In the name of Jesus, I prophesy, release, sow, plant, and cultivate in me a wise and prudent heart to understand my way, discern what to do, and consider what I am doing.

Suggested prayer for your children: In the name of Jesus, I prophesy, release, sow, plant, and cultivate in my sons and daughters [specify their names] wise and prudent hearts to understand their way, discern what to do, and consider what they are doing.

Suggested prayer for other people: In the name of Jesus, I prophesy, release, sow, plant, and cultivate in [specify his or her name] a wise and prudent heart to understand his or her way, discern what to do, and consider what he or she is doing.

11a: The house of the wicked will be destroyed.

Are there places of prostitution, gambling, or other kinds of sin near your home? Prophesy! I remember there was a nightclub close to my house, attended even by teenagers. Whenever I walked in front of that place, I prophesied, "Nightclub, dry up and die!" Do you know what happened? The nightclub closed and became a church! Jesus's name is glorified by our prophetic acts!

Suggested prayer: In the name of Jesus, I prophesy and declare: may all the wicked houses in my city dry and die.

11b: the tent of the upright will flourish.

Suggested prayer: In the name of Jesus, I prophesy and declare: may the homes of all the upright people in my city prosper and experience many blessings.

Suggested prayer for you: Lord Jesus, I open my home life completely for you to make it flourish, prosper, and experience many blessings.

Suggested prayer for your children: Lord Jesus, I bless the homes of my sons and daughters [specify their names] for them to completely open them for you to make them flourish, prosper, and experience many blessings.

Suggested prayer for other people: Lord Jesus, I bless the home of [specify his or her name] for him or her to let it be completely open for you to make it flourish, prosper, and experience many blessings.

14a: The faithless will be fully repaid for their ways.

Suggested prayer: In the name of Jesus, I prophesy and declare: may all the individuals in my city, on TV, and in the government of my country who are unfaithful to God's justice receive retribution for their evil and unfaithful behavior. May they receive what their unfaithful ways deserve. May they get completely tired because of their wicked and unfaithful words, thoughts, and works. May the will of God be done in these situations.

14b: the good man rewarded for his.

Have you been living a life of integrity before God? Then know that he has rewards, peace, and safety for you:

Suggested prayer: Lord Jesus, I open my life completely to your rewards, blessings, peace, safety, and prosperity.

If you know a good man or woman, prophesy on him or her.

Suggested prayer: Lord Jesus, I bless [specify his or her name] to open his or her life completely to your rewards, blessings, peace, safety, and prosperity.

15b: a prudent man gives thought to his steps.

Prudence helps us make right decisions in our projects and plans and helps us see where are going.

Suggested prayer for you: In the name of Jesus, I prophesy, release, sow, plant, and cultivate in me a prudent heart that sees where I step, meditates well in what I am going to do, pays attention in each step, tries to know where I am really going to, and considers my ways carefully.

Suggested prayer for your children: In the name of Jesus, I prophesy, release, sow, plant, and cultivate in my sons and daughters [specify their names] prudent hearts that see where they step, meditate well in what they are going to do, pay attention in each step, try to know where they are really going to, and consider their ways carefully.

Suggested prayer for other people: In the name of Jesus, I prophesy, release, sow, plant, and cultivate in [specify his or her name] a prudent heart that sees where he steps, meditates well in what he is going to do, pays attention in each step, tries to know where he is really going to, and considers his ways carefully.

16a: A wise man fears the LORD and shuns evil.

Suggested prayer for you: In the name of Jesus, I prophesy, release, sow, plant, and cultivate in me a wise heart that is cautious, vigilant, and careful, thinks well before doing something, and avoids evil.

Suggested prayer for your children: In the name of Jesus, I prophesy, release, sow, plant, and cultivate in my sons and daughters [specify their names] wise hearts that are cautious, vigilant, and careful, think well before doing something, and avoid evil.

Suggested prayer for other people: In the name of Jesus, I prophesy, release, sow, plant, and cultivate in [specify his or her name] a wise heart that is cautious, vigilant, and careful, thinks well before doing something, and avoids evil.

> 19: Evil men will bow down in the presence of the good,
> and the wicked at the gates of the righteous.

There are so many evil people trying to harm good people. Prophesy the righteous people's victory.

Suggested prayer: In the name of Jesus, I prophesy and declare: may all the evil and wicked men in my city, on TV, and in the government of my country bow down in the presence of the good and righteous people.

> 21a: He who despises his neighbor sins.

Suggested prayer for you: In the name of Jesus, I prophesy, release, sow, plant, and cultivate in me a mind and heart not to despise or hate those who work, study, or live close to me.

Suggested prayer for other people: In the name of Jesus, I prophesy, release, sow, plant, and cultivate in [specify his or her name] a mind and heart not to despise or hate those who work, study, or live close to him or her.

> 22a: Do not those who plot evil go astray?

Suggested prayer: In the name of Jesus, I prophesy and declare: may all of those in my city, on TV, and in the government of my country who plot evil meet only hindrances, frustrations, and failures in their evil ways, so that they may feel much discouragement in their evil behavior. May they have opportunities to know Jesus and be raised up to do his will.

> 24a: The wealth of the wise is their crown.

Suggested prayer: In the name of Jesus, I prophesy and declare: may all the wise men and women in my city, on TV, and in the government of my country who use their wisdom for God's glory be rewarded with abundant wealth.

25a: A truthful witness saves lives.

Suggested prayer: In the name of Jesus, I prophesy, release, sow, plant, and cultivate on TV and in all the courts in my city truthful witnesses to save lives.

26: He who fears the LORD has a secure fortress, and for his children it will be a refuge.

Suggested prayer: Lord Jesus, I declare you my fortress, my safety, God who clothes me with strength and power. I declare you the refuge and protection of my children.

27: The fear of the LORD is a fountain of life, turning a man from the snares of death.

Suggested prayer for you: In the name of Jesus, I prophesy, release, sow, plant, and cultivate in me the fear of the Lord, which is a fountain of life to turn me from the snares of death.

Suggested prayer for your children: In the name of Jesus, I prophesy, release, sow, plant, and cultivate in my sons and daughters [specify their names] the fear of the Lord, which is a fountain of life to turn them from the snares of death.

Suggested prayer for other people: In the name of Jesus, I prophesy, release, sow, plant, and cultivate in [specify his or her name] the fear of the Lord, which is a fountain of life to turn him or her from the snares of death.

29a: A patient man has great understanding.

Suggested prayer for you: In the name of Jesus, I prophesy, release, sow, plant, and cultivate in me a patient, calm, and intelligent heart that is not irritable.

Suggested prayer for your children: In the name of Jesus, I prophesy, release, sow, plant, and cultivate in my sons and daughters [specify their names] patient, calm, and intelligent hearts that are not irritable.

Suggested prayer for other people: In the name of Jesus, I prophesy, release, sow, plant, and cultivate in [specify his or her name] a patient, calm and intelligent heart that is not irritable.

30a: A heart at peace gives life to the body.

Suggested prayer for you: In the name of Jesus, I prophesy, release, sow, plant, and cultivate in me a calm and healthy heart and mind. Lord Jesus, I open my heart and mind completely to your healing, peace, and health.

Suggested prayer for other people: In the name of Jesus, I prophesy, release, sow, plant, and cultivate in [specify his or her name] a calm and healthy heart and mind. Lord Jesus, I bless him to open his heart and mind completely to your healing, peace, and health.

34a: Righteousness exalts a nation.

Pray for your country!

Suggested prayer: In the name of Jesus, I prophesy, release, sow, plant, and cultivate the righteousness of God in my country, in the government, in the society, etc.

DAY 15

1a: A gentle answer turns away wrath.

Suggested prayer for you: In the name of Jesus, I prophesy, release, sow, plant, and cultivate in me a tongue to give gentle, kind, soft, and calm answers to turn feelings of anger.

Suggested prayer for other people: In the name of Jesus, I prophesy, release, sow, plant, and cultivate in [specify his or her name] a tongue to give gentle, kind, soft, and calm answers to turn feelings of anger.

2a: The tongue of the wise commends knowledge.

Suggested prayer for you: In the name of Jesus, I prophesy, release, sow, plant, and cultivate in me a wise heart and tongue to make my knowledge attractive and express well my knowledge as I open my mouth to speak.

Suggested prayer for other people: In the name of Jesus, I prophesy, release, sow, plant, and cultivate in [specify his or her name] a wise heart and tongue to make his knowledge attractive and express well his knowledge as he opens his mouth to speak.

3: The eyes of the LORD are everywhere, keeping watch on the wicked and the good.

Suggested prayer: In the name of Jesus, I prophesy and declare: may the Lord's eyes be on every place of my city, on TV, and in the government of my country, watching the wicked and the righteous and acting and intervening with justice. May the will of God be done in their situations.

4a: The tongue that brings healing is a tree of life.

Suggested prayer for you: In the name of Jesus, I prophesy, release, sow, plant, and cultivate in me a kind, gentle, comforting, and tranquilizing tongue that will be a tree of life and produce abundant good fruits.

Suggested prayer for other people: In the name of Jesus, I prophesy, release, sow, plant, and cultivate in [specify his or her name] a kind, gentle, comforting, and tranquilizing tongue that will be a tree of life and produce abundant good fruits.

4b: a deceitful tongue crushes the spirit.

Suggested prayer: In the name of Jesus, I prophesy and declare: may the perverted and deceitful tongue of all the sorcerers, witches, and other perverts in my city, on TV, and in the government of my country crush through sadness their own spirits, so that they may feel complete discouragement and abandon their evil, perverted, deceitful, and cruel ways, acts, and words.

5b: whoever heeds correction shows prudence.

This verse may be applied to children and any other person. But it is also useful for us. Everyone needs a reprehension and a life-giving rebuke. God has honor for those who welcome discipline.

Suggested prayer for you: In the name of Jesus, I prophesy, release, sow, plant, and cultivate in me a prudent heart to welcome reprehension, correction, discipline, and life-giving rebukes.

Suggested prayer for your children: In the name of Jesus, I prophesy, release, sow, plant, and cultivate in my sons and daughters [specify their names] prudent hearts to welcome reprehension, correction, discipline, and life-giving rebukes.

Suggested prayer for other people: In the name of Jesus, I prophesy, release, sow, plant, and cultivate in [specify his or her name] a prudent heart to welcome reprehension, correction, discipline, and life-giving rebukes.

6a: The house of the righteous contains great treasure.

If you live in Jesus's righteousness, then know that he has treasures for your home. Treasure or wealth is not necessarily material.

Suggested prayer: Lord Jesus, I open my home completely to your many treasures and wealth.

6b: the income of the wicked brings them trouble.

Suggested prayer: In the name of Jesus, I prophesy and declare: may all the wicked in my city, on TV, and in the government of my country feel completely distressed in their dishonest profits, so that they may completely abandon their dishonesty. May they have opportunities to know Jesus and be raised up to do his will.

7a: The lips of the wise spread knowledge.

This verse may be used to bless all your family.

Suggested prayer for you: In the name of Jesus, I prophesy, release, sow, plant, and cultivate in me a wise heart and lips to say, discreetly and modestly, words that will spread knowledge.

Suggested prayer for your children: In the name of Jesus, I prophesy, release, sow, plant, and cultivate in my sons and daughters [specify their names] wise hearts and lips to say, discreetly and modestly, words that will spread knowledge.

Suggested prayer for other people: In the name of Jesus, I prophesy, release, sow, plant, and cultivate in [specify his or her name] a wise heart and lips to say, discreetly and modestly, words that will spread knowledge.

> 10: Stern discipline awaits him who leaves the path; he
> who hates correction will die.

Such a warning is especially addressed to those leaving the good ways—for example, a Christian becoming a thief, a sorcerer, a gay activist, or a medical doctor who performs abortions.

Suggested prayer: In the name of Jesus, I prophesy and declare: may [specify his or her name] suffer severe and heavy discipline, so that he or she may feel completely distressed for abandoning the good ways. May all of his or her contempt to the reprehension from God's Word dry up and die.

> 13a: A happy heart makes the face cheerful.

Suggested prayer for you: In the name of Jesus, I prophesy, release, sow, plant, and cultivate in me a happy, glad, content, and cheerful heart.

Suggested prayer for other people: In the name of Jesus, I prophesy, release, sow, plant, and cultivate in [specify his or her name] a happy, glad, content, and cheerful heart.

> 14a: The discerning heart seeks knowledge.

Suggested prayer for you: In the name of Jesus, I prophesy, release, sow, plant, and cultivate in me an intelligent mind and a righteous heart to know how to discern and seek the right knowledge to help me. Lord Jesus, I open my heart completely to learn more from what the Lord has to teach me.

Suggested prayer for your children: In the name of Jesus, I prophesy, release, sow, plant, and cultivate in my sons and daughters [specify their names] intelligent minds and righteous hearts to know how to discern and seek the right knowledge to help them.

Suggested prayer for other people: In the name of Jesus, I prophesy, release, sow, plant, and cultivate in [specify his or her name] an intelligent mind and a righteous heart to know how to discern and seek the right knowledge to help him or her.

15b: the cheerful heart has a continual feast.

Suggested prayer for you: In the name of Jesus, I prophesy, release, sow, plant, and cultivate in me a happy, glad, content, cheerful, and quiet heart.

Suggested prayer for other people: In the name of Jesus, I prophesy, release, sow, plant, and cultivate in [specify his or her name] a happy, glad, content, cheerful, and quiet heart.

18b: a patient man calms a quarrel.

Suggested prayer for you: In the name of Jesus, I prophesy, release, sow, plant, and cultivate in me a patient heart that does not get angry easily, controls all its emotions in times of anger, stays calm, and calms down and settles arguments.

Suggested prayer for your children: In the name of Jesus, I prophesy, release, sow, plant, and cultivate in my sons and daughters [specify their names] patient hearts that do not get angry easily, control all their emotions in times of anger, stay calm, and calm down and settle arguments.

Suggested prayer for other people: In the name of Jesus, I prophesy, release, sow, plant, and cultivate in [specify his or her name] a patient heart that does not get angry easily, controls all its emotions in times of anger, stays calm, and calms down and settles arguments.

19b: the path of the upright is a highway.

If you live in Jesus's righteousness, prophesy!

Suggested prayer: In the name of Jesus, I prophesy and declare flat, free, and easy-to-walk highways ahead of me, without difficulties.

20a: A wise son brings joy to his father.

Suggested prayer: In the name of Jesus, I prophesy, release, sow, plant, and cultivate in my sons and daughters [specify their names] wise hearts that will bring me joy.

21b: a man of understanding keeps a straight course.

Suggested prayer for you: In the name of Jesus, I prophesy, release, sow, plant, and cultivate in me a wise heart to make me able to behave with righteousness, intelligence, and justice.

Suggested prayer for your children: In the name of Jesus, I prophesy, release, sow, plant, and cultivate in my sons and daughters [specify their names] wise hearts to make them able to behave with righteousness, intelligence, and justice.

Suggested prayer for other people: In the name of Jesus, I prophesy, release, sow, plant, and cultivate in [specify his or her name] a wise heart to make him or her able to behave with righteousness, intelligence, and justice.

> 22: Plans fail for lack of counsel, but with many advisers
> they succeed.

If you have important plans for your life and work, open yourself up to good advice. Of course, your principal source of advice is the Word of God. But there are also, thanks to God, wonderful brothers and sisters in Christ who can bring you a guiding word that will enlarge your vision for your plans.

Suggested prayer: Lord Jesus, I give full opportunities and free rein for you to bring to me many good counselors. I open my life to your advice through those Christian brothers and sisters.

Suggested prayer for other people, including presidents and national and international authorities: Lord Jesus, I bless [specify their names] for them to give full opportunities and free rein for you to bring many good counselors to them.

> 23: A man finds joy in giving an apt reply—and how
> good is a timely word!

Suggested prayer for you: In the name of Jesus, I prophesy, release, sow, plant, and cultivate in me a heart and mouth as tools of God to give right answers and advice in the right time!

Suggested prayer for your children: In the name of Jesus, I prophesy, release, sow, plant, and cultivate in my sons and daughters [specify their names] hearts and mouths as tools of God to give right answers and advice in the right time!

Suggested prayer for other people, including ministers and evangelists: In the name of Jesus, I prophesy, release, sow, plant, and cultivate in [specify his or her name] a heart and mouth as tools of God to give right answers and advice in the right time!

26a: The LORD detests the thoughts of the wicked.

The minds of the wicked inspire them to defend shamelessly wickedness, adultery, homosexuality, abortion, etc., on TV and in other places. Prophesy!

Suggested prayer: In the name of Jesus, I prophesy and declare: may every thought, plan and intention of perversion of all the wicked in my city, on TV, and in the government of my country fail.

27b: he who hates bribes will live.

Suggested prayer for you: In the name of Jesus, I prophesy, release, sow, plant, and cultivate in me an honest heart to hate bribes.

Suggested prayer for your children: In the name of Jesus, I prophesy, release, sow, plant, and cultivate in my sons and daughters [specify their names] honest hearts to hate bribes.

Suggested prayer for other people: In the name of Jesus, I prophesy, release, sow, plant, and cultivate in [specify his or her name] an honest heart to hate bribes.

Suggested prayer for your city and nation: In the name of Jesus, I prophesy, release, sow, plant, and cultivate in my city and the government of my country authorities who hate bribes.

28a: The heart of the righteous weighs its answers.

Suggested prayer for you: In the name of Jesus, I prophesy, release, sow, plant, and cultivate in me a righteous heart to think and consider very well before answering.

Suggested prayer for your children: In the name of Jesus, I prophesy, release, sow, plant, and cultivate in my sons and daughters [specify their names] righteous hearts to think and consider very well before answering.

Suggested prayer for other people: In the name of Jesus, I prophesy, release, sow, plant, and cultivate in [specify his or her name] a righteous heart to think and consider very well before answering.

30b: good news gives health to the bones.

Today you might receive news that will bring you joy. Who knows? Open yourself up to the surprises from God.

Suggested prayer: Lord Jesus, I open my life completely to your surprises and good news that will cheer, will strengthen, and will make me feel better.

31: He who listens to a life-giving rebuke will be at home among the wise.

Suggested prayer for you: In the name of Jesus, I prophesy, release, sow, plant, and cultivate in me a heart completely open to life-giving rebukes.

Suggested prayer for your children: In the name of Jesus, I prophesy, release, sow, plant, and cultivate in my sons and daughters [specify their names] hearts completely open to life-giving rebukes.

Suggested prayer for other people: In the name of Jesus, I prophesy, release, sow, plant, and cultivate in [specify his or her name] a heart completely open to life-giving rebukes.

Suggested prayer for national and international authorities: In the name of Jesus, I prophesy, release, sow, plant, and cultivate in [specify his or her name] a heart completely open to life-giving rebukes.

32b: whoever heeds correction gains understanding.

Suggested prayer for you: In the name of Jesus, I prophesy, release, sow, plant, and cultivate in me an open heart to hear and welcome correction.

Suggested prayer for your children: In the name of Jesus, I prophesy, release, sow, plant, and cultivate in my sons and daughters [specify their names] open hearts to hear and welcome correction.

Suggested prayer for other people: In the name of Jesus, I prophesy, release, sow, plant, and cultivate in [specify his or her name] an open heart to hear and welcome correction.

Suggested prayer for national and international authorities: In the name of Jesus, I prophesy, release, sow, plant, and cultivate in [specify his or her name] an open heart to hear and welcome correction.

33a: The fear of the LORD teaches a man wisdom.

Suggested prayer for you: In the name of Jesus, I prophesy, release, sow, plant, and cultivate in me the fear of the Lord to teach me wisdom.

Suggested prayer for your children: In the name of Jesus, I prophesy, release, sow, plant, and cultivate in my sons and daughters [specify their names] the fear of the Lord to teach them wisdom.

Suggested prayer for other people: In the name of Jesus, I prophesy, release, sow, plant, and cultivate in [specify his or her name] the fear of the Lord to teach him or her wisdom.

Suggested prayer for other people: In the name of Jesus, I prophesy, release, sow, plant, and cultivate in [specify his or her name] the fear of the Lord to teach him or her wisdom.

Additional suggested prayer: In the name of Jesus, I prophesy, release, sow, plant, and cultivate the fear of the Lord in all authorities in my city, the government of my country, and in everybody who works in the media to teach them wisdom.

1: To man belong the plans of the heart, but from the LORD comes the reply of the tongue.

Place all the purposes of your heart before Jesus and give him opportunities to speak and guide.

Suggested prayer for you: Lord Jesus, I deliver and place into your hands my plan [specify it], so that the Lord may act, decide, and intervene mightily in that situation. I give full opportunities and free rein for you to open your lips and to give your answer and final word in that situation. I give you full opportunities and free rein to make my plans come true.

Suggested prayer for your children: Lord Jesus, I deliver and place into your hands my children's plans [specify your children's names and their plans], so that the Lord may act, decide, and intervene mightily in that situation. I bless them to give full opportunities and free rein for you to open your lips and to give your answer and final word in that situation. I bless them to give you full opportunities and free rein to make their plans come true.

Suggested prayer for other people: Lord Jesus, I deliver and place into your hands the plan of [specify his or her name], so that the Lord may act, decide, and intervene mightily in that situation. I bless him or her to give full opportunities and free rein to open your lips and to give your answer and final word in that situation.

Suggested prayer for national and international authorities: Lord Jesus, I deliver and place into your hands the plan of [specify his or her name], so that the Lord may act, decide, and intervene mightily in that situation. I bless them to give full opportunities and free rein for you to open your lips and to give your answer and final word in that situation.

> 2: All a man's ways seem innocent to him, but motives
> are weighed by the LORD.

Does someone in your family (an adult son, for instance) think everything he does is right and is not able to see the reality? Prophesy!

Suggested prayer: Lord Jesus, I deliver and place [add the person's name] into your hands in his or her attitude of seeing all his or her ways as pure and in his or her attitude of thinking that everything he or she does is right. I give full opportunities and free rein for you to judge, weigh, and evaluate his or her reasons and intentions and show him or her the truth.

Suggested prayer for national and international authorities: Lord Jesus, I deliver and place [add their names] into your hands in their attitude of seeing all their ways as pure and in their attitude of thinking that everything that they do is right. I give full opportunities and free rein for the Lord to judge, weigh, and evaluate their reasons and intentions and show them.

> 3: Commit to the LORD whatever you do, and your
> plans will succeed.

Remember to place before Jesus everything you do.

Suggested prayer: Lord Jesus, I consecrate, deliver, and place into your hands all that I am doing [specify it], and I give full opportunities and free rein for the Lord to establish my purposes and make my plans prosperous and successful.

> 5: The LORD detests all the proud of heart. Be sure of this: They will not go unpunished.

Do you see the wicked showing arrogance, mocking God's principles, and shamelessly defending wickedness, adultery, homosexuality, abortion, etc., as if they didn't have to give an account to God? That is arrogance against the laws of God. Prophesy! Agree with God, because he knows the kind of punishment the proud mockers need. Just prophesy. When the proud mockers receive punishment for their wickedness, the inexperienced learn a lesson. If they are not punished, the inexperienced will imitate their mockery and wrong life. God doesn't want that. What about you?

Suggested prayer: In the name of Jesus, I prophesy and declare: may the mocking, proud, perverse, and distorted mind and heart of all the wicked in my city, on TV, and in the government of my country receive discipline and correction, not praises. I prophesy and declare: may all those proud mockers be taught, through discipline and correction from God, not to mock God's principles and not to promote evil.

> 6b: through the fear of the LORD a man avoids evil.

Suggested prayer for you: In the name of Jesus, I prophesy, release, sow, plant, and cultivate in me the fear of the Lord to help me avoid sin and keep away from every appearance of evil.

Suggested prayer for your children: In the name of Jesus, I prophesy, release, sow, plant, and cultivate in my sons and daughters [specify their names] the fear of the Lord to help them avoid sin and keep away from every appearance of evil.

Suggested prayer for other people: In the name of Jesus, I prophesy, release, sow, plant, and cultivate in [specify his or her name] the fear of the Lord to help him or her avoid sin and keep away from every appearance of evil.

> 9: In his heart a man plans his course, but the LORD determines his steps.

If you are making important plans (marriage, for instance), remember to place everything before Jesus.

Suggested prayer for you: Lord Jesus, I deliver and place into your hands all that I am planning and deciding to do [specify it], so that the Lord may intervene and show and establish your will. I give full opportunities and free rein for you to guide and determine my steps and actions and decide where I should go and what I should do.

Suggested prayer for your children: Lord Jesus, I deliver and place into your hands all that my sons and daughters [specify their names] are planning and deciding to do, so that the Lord may intervene and show and establish your will. I bless them for them to give full opportunities and free rein for you to guide and determine their steps and actions and decide where they should go and what they should do.

By faith, you can pray for the president of your nation:

Suggested prayer: Lord Jesus, I deliver and place into your hands all that the president is planning and deciding to do [about Israel, Christian refugees, abortion, family, homeschooling, homosexuality], so that the Lord may intervene and show and establish your will. I bless him to give full opportunities and free rein for you to guide and determine his steps and actions and decide where he should go and what he should do.

10: The lips of a king speak as an oracle, and his mouth
should not betray justice.

Suggested prayer for your president: In the name of Jesus, I prophesy, release, sow, plant, and cultivate in the president of my nation a mouth that will not betray God's justice, not deciding against the unborn, the family, homeschooling, and Israel. May he have opportunities to know Jesus and be raised up to do his will and defend God's justice, including the unborn, the family, homeschooling, and Israel.

12: Kings detest wrongdoing, for a throne is established
through righteousness.

Suggested prayer for your president: In the name of Jesus, I prophesy, release, sow, plant, and cultivate in the president of my nation a righteous heart to detest wrongdoing and not to tolerate abortion, anti-Semitism, socialism, gay activism, and other evils. I prophesy, release, sow, plant, and cultivate in my nation a righteous government. May God's righteousness make the government of my country strong and powerful to do God's will and defend God's justice.

13: Kings take pleasure in honest lips; they value a man
who speaks the truth.

Suggested prayer for your president: In the name of Jesus, I prophesy, release, sow, plant, and cultivate in the president of my nation a heart to take pleasure in honest lips and value people who speak the truth. May he have pleasure and pay attention only to the advice of honest counselors.

17: The highway of the upright avoids evil; he who
guards his way guards his life.

Suggested prayer for you: In the name of Jesus, I prophesy, release, sow, plant, and cultivate in me a righteous heart to take care of my ways, acts, words, and thoughts and to watch attentively where I am going and to avoid every appearance of evil.

Suggested prayer for your children: In the name of Jesus, I prophesy, release, sow, plant, and cultivate in my sons and daughters [specify their names] righteous hearts to take care of their ways, acts, words, and thoughts and to watch attentively where they are going and to avoid every appearance of evil.

Suggested prayer for other people: In the name of Jesus, I prophesy, release, sow, plant, and cultivate in [specify his or her name] a righteous heart to take care of his or her ways, acts, words, and thoughts and to watch attentively where he or she is going and to avoid every appearance of evil.

> 20: Whoever gives heed to instruction prospers, and blessed is he who trusts in the LORD.

Another translation says, "Whoever gives attention to the LORD'S word prospers, and blessed is the person who trusts the LORD" (GW). Have you lived as Joshua 1:7–8? Do you trust in Jesus? Then open yourself to what God has in store for your life.

Suggested prayer for you: In the name of Jesus, I prophesy, release, sow, plant, and cultivate in me a heart and ears to give much attention to God's Word and to the voice of the Holy Spirit. Lord Jesus, I open my life completely to your blessings, prosperity, and success.

Suggested prayer for your children: In the name of Jesus, I prophesy, release, sow, plant, and cultivate in my sons and daughters [specify their names] hearts and ears to give much attention to God's Word and to the voice of the Holy Spirit.

Suggested prayer for other people: In the name of Jesus, I prophesy, release, sow, plant, and cultivate in [specify his or her name] a heart and ears to give much attention to God's Word and to the voice of the Holy Spirit.

21: The wise in heart are called discerning, and pleasant words promote instruction.

Suggested prayer for you: In the name of Jesus, I prophesy, release, sow, plant, and cultivate in me a wise and prudent heart and a mouth to speak kindly and sensibly and promote instruction.

Suggested prayer for other people: In the name of Jesus, I prophesy, release, sow, plant, and cultivate in [specify his or her name] a wise and prudent heart and a mouth to speak kindly and sensibly and promote instruction.

22b: folly brings punishment to fools.

Do you see fools shamelessly bragging about adultery, homosexuality, abortion, etc.? Prophesy!

Suggested prayer: In the name of Jesus, I prophesy and declare: may all the fools in my city, on TV, and in the government of my country receive punishment for their perverted behavior and arrogant and foolish words. I deliver and place them into the just hands of God.

23: A wise man's heart guides his mouth, and his lips promote instruction.

Suggested prayer for you: In the name of Jesus, I prophesy, release, sow, plant, and cultivate in me a wise heart to teach, control, and guide my mouth. I prophesy, release, sow, plant, and cultivate in me lips to promote instruction.

Suggested prayer for other people: In the name of Jesus, I prophesy, release, sow, plant, and cultivate in [specify his or her name] a wise heart to teach, control, and guide his or her mouth. I prophesy, release, sow, plant, and cultivate in him or her lips to promote instruction.

24: Pleasant words are a honeycomb, sweet to the soul
and healing to the bones.

Suggested prayer for you: In the name of Jesus, I prophesy, release, sow, plant, and cultivate in my tongue pleasing words as a honeycomb, for encouraging, cheering up, and healing people and their souls and bodies.

32: Better a patient man than a warrior, a man who
controls his temper than one who takes a city.

Suggested prayer for you: In the name of Jesus, I prophesy, release, sow, plant, and cultivate in me a patient heart to keep me under control and to control and master my feelings and emotions in the hard.

Suggested prayer for your children: In the name of Jesus, I prophesy, release, sow, plant, and cultivate in my sons and daughters [specify their names] patient hearts to keep them under control and to control and master their feelings and emotions in the hard situations and not to get angry easily.

Suggested prayer for other people: In the name of Jesus, I prophesy, release, sow, plant, and cultivate in [specify his or her name] a patient heart to keep him or her under control and to control and master his or her feelings and emotions in the hard situations and not to get angry easily.

33: The lot is cast into the lap, but its every decision is
from the LORD.

When you have to make decisions, place all the purposes of your heart before Jesus, and give him opportunities to guide and decide.

Suggested prayer for you: Lord Jesus, I deliver and place into your hands my plans and decisions [specify them], so that the Lord may act, decide, and intervene mightily in those situations. I give full opportunities and free rein for you to determine and guide your answers and decisions and the result of everything. I give you full opportunities and free rein to speak in those situations.

Suggested prayer for your children: Lord Jesus, I deliver and place into your hands my children's plans [specify your children's names and their plans], so that the Lord may act, decide, and intervene mightily in those situations. I bless them to give full opportunities and free rein for you to determine and guide your answers and decisions and the result of everything. I bless them to give you full opportunities and free rein to speak in those situations.

Suggested prayer for other people: Lord Jesus, I deliver and place into your hands the plan of [specify his or her name], so that the Lord may act, decide, and intervene mightily in that situation. I bless him or her to give full opportunities and free rein for you to determine and guide your answers and decisions and the result of everything. I bless him or her to give you full opportunities and free rein to speak in those situations.

Suggested prayer for national and international authorities: Lord Jesus, I deliver and place into your hands the plan of [specify his or her name], so that the Lord may act, decide, and intervene mightily in that situation. I bless him or her to give full opportunities and free rein for you to determine and guide your answers and decisions and the result of everything. I bless him or her to give you full opportunities and free rein to speak in those situations.

3: The crucible for silver and the furnace for gold, but
the LORD tests the heart.

Suggested prayer for you: Lord Jesus, I give full opportunities and free rein to purify with fire my heart.

Suggested prayer for other people: Lord Jesus, I bless [specify his or her name] for you to purify with fire his or her heart.

6: Children's children are a crown to the aged, and parents are the pride of their children.

Suggested prayer: Lord Jesus, I give full opportunities and free rein for the Lord to make me the pride and glory of my children. In the name of Jesus, I prophesy, release, sow, plant, and cultivate in my family grandchildren who will be a crown for me.

9: He who covers over an offense promotes love.

Suggested prayer for you: In the name of Jesus, I prophesy, release, sow, plant, and cultivate in me a prudent heart to pay no attention to the insults and offenses people perpetrate against me.

Suggested prayer for other people: In the name of Jesus, I prophesy, release, sow, plant, and cultivate in in [specify his or her name] a prudent heart to pay no attention to the insults and offenses people perpetrate against him.

10: A rebuke impresses a man of discernment more than
a hundred lashes a fool.

Suggested prayer for you: In the name of Jesus, I prophesy, release, sow, plant, and cultivate in me a spiritually intelligent heart open to receive correction and rebuke from the Lord.

Suggested prayer for your children: In the name of Jesus, I prophesy, release, sow, plant, and cultivate in my sons and daughters [specify their names] spiritually intelligent hearts open to receive correction and rebuke from the Lord.

Suggested prayer for other people: In the name of Jesus, I prophesy, release, sow, plant, and cultivate in [specify his or her name] a spiritually intelligent heart open to receive correction and rebuke from the Lord.

11: An evil man is bent only on rebellion; a merciless
official will be sent against him.

The Septuagint says: "Every bad man stirs up strifes: but the Lord will send out against him an unmerciful messenger" (Brenton).

Suggested prayer: In the name of Jesus, I prophesy and declare: may the Lord send a merciless messenger to all the bad, rebel, and evil individuals who want to upset the country and establish laws against the ethical values of God. May the will of God be done in these situations.

15: Acquitting the guilty and condemning the
innocent—the LORD detests them both.

It is not necessary to mention the sad reality that there are dishonest lawyers and judges. But we can intervene prophetically. You know God's opinion: he doesn't want the guilty to be absolved, and he doesn't want the innocent to be condemned.

Suggested prayer: In the name of Jesus, I deliver and place into the just hands of God the situations in my city in which dishonest lawyers and judges want to acquit criminals and condemn the innocent. In the name of Jesus, I prophesy and declare: may all those lawyers and judges be disciplined as the Lord has already determined in his Word. I prophesy and declare: may all the criminals be totally condemned, and may all the innocent be defended and absolved. I deliver and place them into the just hands of God. May God's will be done in those situations.

20: A man of perverse heart does not prosper; he whose tongue is deceitful falls into trouble.

Do you see the fools shamelessly defending sins as adultery, homosexuality, abortion, etc.? Prophesy! Consider it: if a fool falls into anguish and distress every time he uses his tongue for evil, he will get tired of using his tongue for evil! At the same time, pray for God to have mercy of those who are involved in those sins, so that they may experience deliverance and salvation in Jesus Christ

Suggested prayer: In the name of Jesus, I prophesy and declare: may all individuals of perverse heart in my city, on TV, and in the government of my country not prosper and have no contentment in their deceitful words. May their deceitful tongues fall in distress and agony, so that they abandon perversion. I place them in the just hands of God.

22a: A cheerful heart is good medicine.

Suggested prayer for you: In the name of Jesus, I prophesy, release, sow, plant, and cultivate in me a cheerful and well-disposed heart to promote my healing and health.

Suggested prayer for your children: In the name of Jesus, I prophesy, release, sow, plant, and cultivate in my sons and daughters [specify their

names] cheerful and well-disposed hearts to promote their healing and health.

Suggested prayer for other people: In the name of Jesus, I prophesy, release, sow, plant, and cultivate in [specify his or her name] a cheerful and well- disposed heart to promote his or her healing and health.

23: A wicked man accepts a bribe in secret to pervert the course of justice.

Another translation says: "Corrupt judges accept secret bribes, and then justice is not done" (GNT).

Suggested prayer: In the name of Jesus, I deliver and place into the just hands of God the situations in my city in which judges, lawyers, politicians, and other authorities are involved in bribes. May the Lord intervene mightily in those situations. May all secret acts of bribe and corruption be frustrated and fail. May God's will be done in those situations.

24a: A discerning man keeps wisdom in view.

Suggested prayer for you: In the name of Jesus, I prophesy, release, sow, plant, and cultivate in me an intelligent, disciplined, and calm heart to keep me under control and before acting and speaking, always carefully consider the wisest and the most discreet way to act and speak.

Suggested prayer for your children: In the name of Jesus, I prophesy, release, sow, plant, and cultivate in my sons and daughters [specify their names] intelligent, disciplined, and calm hearts to keep them under control and before acting and speaking, always carefully consider the wisest and the most discreet way to act and speak.

Suggested prayer for other people: In the name of Jesus, I prophesy, release, sow, plant, and cultivate in [specify his or her name] an intelligent, disciplined, and calm heart to keep him or her under control and before acting and speaking, always carefully consider the wisest and the most discreet way to act and speak.

> 26: It is not good to punish an innocent man, or to flog
> officials for their integrity.

I have never worked in a political job, but I know that in the political circles there is so much corruption and deception that many times corrupt individuals try to put on the honest leaders the image of what they are. Then those who are dishonest get an image of honesty. God does not want that.

Suggested prayer: In the name of Jesus, I deliver and place into the just hands of God the situations in my city and country in which innocent leaders and other innocent people are suffering injustice. May all those innocent leaders and people be honored, not repressed. May God's justice prevail in those situations. May God's will be done in those situations.

> 27: A man of knowledge uses words with restraint, and
> a man of understanding is even-tempered.

Suggested prayer for you: In the name of Jesus, I prophesy, release, sow, plant, and cultivate in me a discreet and intelligent heart to stay always calm and speak little, control the words, and avoid hard words.

Suggested prayer for your children: In the name of Jesus, I prophesy, release, sow, plant, and cultivate in my sons and daughters [specify their names] discreet and intelligent hearts to stay always calm and speak little, control the words, and avoid hard words.

Suggested prayer for other people: In the name of Jesus, I prophesy, release, sow, plant, and cultivate in [specify his or her name] a discreet and intelligent heart to stay always calm and speak little, control the words, and avoid hard words.

> 28: Even a fool is thought wise if he keeps silent, and discerning if he holds his tongue.

Suggested prayer for you: In the name of Jesus, I prophesy, release, sow, plant, and cultivate in me a prudent heart to know how to master my tongue, keep my lips closed, and be silent when necessary.

Suggested prayer for your children: In the name of Jesus, I prophesy, release, sow, plant, and cultivate in my sons and daughters [specify their names] prudent hearts to know how to master their tongues, keep their lips closed, and be silent when necessary.

Suggested prayer for other people: In the name of Jesus, I prophesy, release, sow, plant, and cultivate in [specify his or her name] a prudent heart to know how to master his or her tongue, keep his or her lips closed, and be silent when necessary.

4b: the fountain of wisdom is a bubbling brook.

Suggested prayer: Lord Jesus, I open my innermost being to you, and I give full opportunities and free rein for to make your fountain of wisdom as a bubbling brook in me.

> 5: It is not good to be partial to the wicked or to deprive the innocent of justice.

It is not necessary to mention the sad reality that there are dishonest lawyers and judges. But we can intervene prophetically, because God doesn't want the wicked to be favored and the innocent to suffer a wrong decision against their cause.

Suggested prayer: In the name of Jesus, I deliver and I place into the just hands of God all the situations in my city, on TV, and in the government of my country in which lawyers, judges, and other authorities and leaders want to be partial to the wicked and deprive the innocent of justice. I prophesy and declare: may all the criminals be totally condemned and may the innocent be protected and receive justice. I deliver and put all those situations into the just hands of God, and I curse every partiality toward the wicked. I bless all the authorities and leaders so that they don't respect or favor the wicked and so they may help the innocent receive justice. May the wicked be condemned and may the innocent receive justice, in the name of Jesus! May the will of God be done in their situations.

> 6: A fool's lips bring him strife, and his mouth invites
> a beating.

Individuals who despise the wisdom of the Word of God defy in their advocacy of wickedness in society. We see people of that kind shamelessly defending abortion, adultery, homosexuality, etc. But the Word of God shows that their mouths need a beating to correct them. Let us help them, prophetically.

Suggested prayer: In the name of Jesus, I prophesy, declare, and release discipline, lashes, and correction in the mouths of all the fools and sorcerers in my city, on TV, and in the government of my country so that they may not use their words to fight and quarrel on behalf of perversions. May their mouths be corrected and disciplined. May the will of God be done in their mouths.

> 7: A fool's mouth is his undoing, and his lips are a snare
> to his soul.

See the orientation of the previous verse.

Suggested prayer: In the name of Jesus, I prophesy and declare: may the words of all the fools in my city, on TV, and in the government of my country praising sin be to them reason of sadness, shame, and confusion, not pride and pleasure.

> 12b: humility comes before honor.

Suggested prayer for you: In the name of Jesus, I prophesy, release, sow, plant, and cultivate in me a humble heart.

Suggested prayer for your children: In the name of Jesus, I prophesy, release, sow, plant, and cultivate in my sons and daughters [specify their names] humble hearts.

Suggested prayer for other people: In the name of Jesus, I prophesy, release, sow, plant, and cultivate in [specify his or her name] a humble heart.

> 13: He who answers before listening—that is his folly
> and his shame.

Suggested prayer for you: In the name of Jesus, I prophesy, release, sow, plant, and cultivate in me a prudent, discreet, calm, and patient heart to know how to be quiet and hear and think carefully before giving an answer.

Suggested prayer for your children: In the name of Jesus, I prophesy, release, sow, plant, and cultivate in my sons and daughters [specify their names] prudent, discreet, calm, and patient hearts to know how to be quiet and hear and think carefully before giving an answer.

Suggested prayer for other people: In the name of Jesus, I prophesy, release, sow, plant, and cultivate in [specify his or her name] a prudent, discreet, calm, and patient heart to know how to be quiet and hear and think carefully before giving an answer.

> 15: The heart of the discerning acquires knowledge; the
> ears of the wise seek it out.

Suggested prayer for you: In the name of Jesus, I prophesy, release, sow, plant, and cultivate in me a prudent and discreet heart open to learn from the Lord and gain more knowledge. I prophesy, release, sow, plant, and cultivate in me ears attentive to Holy Spirit's voice.

Suggested prayer for your children: In the name of Jesus, I prophesy, release, sow, plant, and cultivate in my sons and daughters [specify their names] prudent and discreet hearts open to learn from the Lord and gain more knowledge. I prophesy, release, sow, plant, and cultivate in them ears attentive to Holy Spirit's voice.

Suggested prayer for other people: In the name of Jesus, I prophesy, release, sow, plant, and cultivate in [specify his or her name] a prudent and discreet heart open to learn from the Lord and gain more knowledge. I prophesy, release, sow, plant, and cultivate in him or her ears attentive to Holy Spirit's voice.

> 21: The tongue has the power of life and death, and those who love it will eat its fruit.

In this book, you are learning how to release the Word of God for the accomplishment of the will of God in many situations and people. The Word of God has power and doesn't return empty. But that same Word assures us that *all people's tongues have the power to release life and death through words.* While you are using your tongue to bless your own life, your family, other people, and your city, there are people who complain without ceasing and say that everything is going bad and that nothing goes right. People like these may be uttering careless words regarding you and your work, ministry and family, without noticing that those words may cause damage. But there is protection. You can daily cover yourself with Jesus's blood and annul every cursed word against you and your family. I daily do that. Besides, I annul any careless word that I might have released without thinking before speaking. When I see that I uttered a careless word to or about someone, immediately I ask for forgiveness and annul that word. We have need, besides asking forgiveness, to annul any complaint and negative word released from our lips.

Suggested prayer: In the name of Jesus, I burn and annul every cursed word thrown today against me and against my family from words of my lips and of the lips of other people.

Suggested prayer for you: Lord Jesus, I prophesy, consecrate, release, sow, plant, and cultivate in me a tongue to release words that will bring life to your purposes and death to the purposes of the defeated one.

Suggested prayer for your children: Lord Jesus, I prophesy, consecrate, release, sow, plant, and cultivate in my sons and daughters [specify their names] tongues to release words that will bring life to your purposes and death to the purposes of the defeated one.

Suggested prayer for other people: Lord Jesus, I prophesy, consecrate, release, sow, plant, and cultivate in [specify his or her name] a tongue to release words that will bring life to your purposes and death to the purposes of the defeated one.

> 22: He who finds a wife finds what is good and receives favor from the LORD.

If you are single, let Jesus bless your life.

Suggested prayer: Lord Jesus, I open my life completely to your superabundant grace for marriage. I give you full opportunities and free rein to pour out on me your excellent grace and bless me for me to find my wife. Lord Jesus, I give full opportunities and free rein for to give me a prudent wife as a gift. May the will of God be done in my life.

Suggested prayer for your sons: Lord Jesus, I bless my sons so that they may receive your favor, grace, and blessing to find their wives.

Suggested prayer for your daughters: Lord Jesus, I bless my daughters so that only men under your favor may find them as wives.

2: It is not good to have zeal without knowledge, nor to be hasty and miss the way.

Suggested prayer for you: In the name of Jesus, I prophesy, release, sow, plant, and cultivate in me a heart to not let me act without thinking, so that I may have zeal and knowledge in what I do. I prophesy, release, sow, plant, and cultivate in me a calm and patient heart to not be hasty in my words and actions.

Suggested prayer for your children: In the name of Jesus, I prophesy, release, sow, plant, and cultivate in my sons and daughters [specify their names] hearts to not let them act without thinking, so that they may have zeal and knowledge in what they do. I prophesy, release, sow, plant, and cultivate in them calm and patient hearts to not be hasty in their words and actions.

Suggested prayer for other people: In the name of Jesus, I prophesy, release, sow, plant, and cultivate in [specify his or her name] a heart to not let him or her act without thinking, so that he or she may have zeal and knowledge in what he or she does. I prophesy, release, sow, plant, and cultivate in him or her a calm and patient heart to not be hasty in his or her words and actions.

5: A false witness will not go unpunished, and he who pours out lies will not go free.

God doesn't want any lying witness to go without punishment. Let us agree with him.

Suggested prayer: In the name of Jesus, I prophesy and declare: may all the false witnesses in my city, on TV, and in the government of my country not go without punishment.

> 8: He who gets wisdom loves his own soul; he who cherishes understanding prospers.

Do you want to prosper? Always read and meditate in the Word of God and let the Holy Spirit guide you through the reading of that Word. (Also see Joshua 1:7–8.)

Suggested prayer for you: In the name of Jesus, I prophesy, release, sow, plant, and cultivate in me a completely open heart to love, meditate on, and remember the Word of God.

Suggested prayer for your children: In the name of Jesus, I prophesy, release, sow, plant, and cultivate in my sons and daughters [specify their names] completely open hearts to love, meditate on, and remember the Word of God.

Suggested prayer for other people: In the name of Jesus, I prophesy, release, sow, plant, and cultivate in [specify his or her name] a completely open heart to love, meditate on, and remember the Word of God.

> 9: A false witness will not go unpunished, and he who pours out lies will perish.

The repetition of that passage shows that God is absolutely against every kind of lying witness.

Suggested prayer: In the name of Jesus, I prophesy and declare: may all the false witnesses in my city, on TV, and in the government of my country not go without punishment.

10a: It is not fitting for a fool to live in luxury.

Suggested prayer: In the name of Jesus, I prophesy and declare: may all the fools and sorcerers in my city, on TV, and in the government of my country who despise the principles of God will not be able to live in luxury or in material comfort.

11: A man's wisdom gives him patience; it is to his glory
to overlook an offense.

Suggested prayer for you: In the name of Jesus, I prophesy, release, sow, plant, and cultivate in me a wise, discreet, and patient heart to pay no attention to the insults and offenses that the people commit against me. In my attitude of not paying attention to insults, I give full opportunities and free rein for the Lord to honor me with his honor.

Suggested prayer for your children: In the name of Jesus, I prophesy, release, sow, plant, and cultivate in my sons and daughters [specify their names] wise, discreet, and patient hearts to pay no attention to the insults and offenses that the people commit against them.

Suggested prayer for other people: In the name of Jesus, I prophesy, release, sow, plant, and cultivate in [specify his or her name] a wise, discreet, and patient heart to pay no attention to the insults and offenses that the people commit against him or her.

14b: a prudent wife is from the LORD.

God has a special inheritance for the single men: a prudent wife! If you are single, prophesy:

Suggested prayer: Lord Jesus, I open my life completely for you to send me your inheritance of a wise, prudent, understanding and intelligent wife. I give full opportunities and free rein for you to give me as your gift a wise wife suited to me.

Suggested prayer for your daughters: Lord Jesus, I bless my daughters. In the name of Jesus, I prophesy, release, sow, plant, and cultivate in my daughters [specify their names] wise, discreet, prudent, and patient hearts. I consecrate them to be inherited, as wives, by righteous and wise men.

> 18: Discipline your son, for in that there is hope; do not
> be a willing party to his death.

Another version says: "Discipline your children while they are young enough to learn. If you don't, you are helping them destroy themselves" (18a GNT).

Suggested prayer for you: In the name of Jesus, I prophesy, release, sow, plant, and cultivate in me a wise, intelligent, and prudent heart to discipline, train, and correct my children with words and with the rod.

Suggested prayer for other people: In the name of Jesus, I prophesy, release, sow, plant, and cultivate in [specify his or her name] a wise, intelligent, and prudent heart to discipline, train, and correct his or her children with words and with the rod.

> 20: Listen to advice and accept instruction, and in the
> end you will be wise.

Help your children with good advice and instructions, and sow in them hearts to hear and pay attention. Your responsibility is to advise them the way that the Lord would advise them.

Suggested prayer for your children: In the name of Jesus, I prophesy, release, sow, plant, and cultivate in my sons and daughters [specify their names] hearts and ears open to good advice, suggestions, corrections, and instructions.

Suggested prayer for other people: In the name of Jesus, I prophesy, release, sow, plant, and cultivate in [specify his or her name] a heart and ears open to good advice, suggestions, corrections, and instructions.

> 21: Many are the plans in a man's heart, but it is the LORD's purpose that prevails.

When you make your plans (marriage, for instance), put *all the purposes of your heart* before Jesus and give him opportunities to guide.

Suggested prayer for you: Lord Jesus, I deliver and place into your hands all the purposes of my heart (specify them), so that your purposes for me prevail and stay unshakable. I give full opportunities and free rein for you to accomplish, confirm, and strengthen all the Lord has already decided, planned, and determined for me. May your projects, plans, and strategies for me prevail and be established, in the name of Jesus!

Suggested prayer for your children: Lord Jesus, I deliver and place into your hands all the purposes of the heart of my sons and daughters [specify their names], so that your purposes for them prevail and stay unshakable. May your projects, plans, and strategies for them prevail and be established, in the name of Jesus!

Suggested prayer for other people: Lord Jesus, I deliver and place into your hands all the purposes of the heart of [specify his or her name], so that your purposes for him or her prevail and stay unshakable. May your projects, plans, and strategies for him or her prevail and be established, in the name of Jesus!

Suggested prayer for national and international authorities: Lord Jesus, I deliver and place into your hands all the purposes of the heart of [specify his or her name], so that your purposes for him or her prevail and stay unshakable.

May your projects, plans, and strategies for him or her prevail and be established, in the name of Jesus!

> 23: The fear of the LORD leads to life: Then one rests content, untouched by trouble.

Suggested prayer for you: In the name of Jesus, I prophesy, release, sow, plant, and cultivate in me a heart to love and fear the Lord.

Suggested prayer for your children: In the name of Jesus, I prophesy, release, sow, plant, and cultivate in my sons and daughters [specify their names] hearts to love and fear the Lord.

Suggested prayer for other people: In the name of Jesus, I prophesy, release, sow, plant, and cultivate in [specify his or her name] a heart to love and fear the Lord.

Suggested prayer for national and international authorities: In the name of Jesus, I prophesy, release, sow, plant, and cultivate in [specify his or her name] a heart to love and fear the Lord.

> 25a: Flog a mocker, and the simple will learn prudence.

Do you see the wicked shamelessly defending wickedness, adultery, homosexuality, abortion, etc., and still receiving praises on TV? That is to mock the Word of God. Prophesy! Agree with God, because he knows the kind of punishment that mockers need. Just prophesy. When the proud mockers receive punishment for their sins, the inexperienced learn a lesson. If they are not punished, the inexperienced will imitate their mockery and wicked lives. God doesn't want that. What about you?

Suggested prayer: In the name of Jesus, I prophesy and declare: may the mocking, proud, perverse, and distorted mind and heart of all the wicked in my city, on TV, and in the government of my country receive discipline and correction, not praises. I prophesy, declare, and release discipline and correction of God to those mockers, so that their evil conduct may be detained and so that the inexperienced may learn how to be prudent.

> 29: Penalties are prepared for mockers, and beatings for the backs of fools.

Do you see the wicked shamelessly defending wickedness, adultery, homosexuality, abortion, etc., and still receiving praises on TV? That is to mock the Word of God. Prophesy! Agree with God, because he knows the kind of punishment that mockers need. Just prophesy.

Suggested prayer: In the name of Jesus, I prophesy and declare: may all the proud mockers, sorcerers, and fools in my city, on TV, and in the government of my country receive punishments and lashes. I deliver and place them into the just hands of God. May the will of God be done in their lives.

DAY 20

3a: It is to a man's honor to avoid strife.

Suggested prayer for you: In the name of Jesus, I prophesy, release, sow, plant, and cultivate in me a wise heart to keep me aloof from quarrels and help me avoid strife.

Suggested prayer for your children: In the name of Jesus, I prophesy, release, sow, plant, and cultivate in my sons and daughters [specify their names] wise hearts to keep them aloof from quarrels and help them avoid strife.

Suggested prayer for other people: In the name of Jesus, I prophesy, release, sow, plant, and cultivate in [specify his or her name] a wise heart to keep him or her aloof from quarrels and help him or her avoid strife.

Suggested prayer for national and international authorities: In the name of Jesus, I prophesy, release, sow, plant, and cultivate in [specify his or her name] a wise heart to keep him or her aloof from quarrels and help him or her avoid strife.

5: The purposes of a man's heart are deep waters, but a man of understanding draws them out.

Suggested prayer for you: In the name of Jesus, I prophesy, release, sow, plant, and cultivate in me a heart full of wisdom and prudence to draw out the deepest purposes and help me understand the deepest thoughts and intentions of my heart.

Suggested prayer for your children: In the name of Jesus, I prophesy, release, sow, plant, and cultivate in my sons and daughters [specify their names] hearts full of wisdom and prudence to draw out the deepest purposes and help them understand the deepest thoughts and intentions of their hearts.

Suggested prayer for other people: In the name of Jesus, I prophesy, release, sow, plant, and cultivate in [specify his or her name] a heart full of wisdom and prudence to draw out the deepest purposes and help him or her understand the deepest thoughts and intentions of his or her heart.

> 6: Many a man claims to have unfailing love, but a faithful man who can find?

Suggested prayer for you: In the name of Jesus, I prophesy, release, sow, plant, and cultivate in my life faithful and trustworthy friends.

Suggested prayer for your children: In the name of Jesus, I prophesy, release, sow, plant, and cultivate faithful and trustworthy friends in the lives of my sons and daughters [specify their names].

> 7: The righteous man leads a blameless life; blessed are his children after him.

Suggested prayer: In the name of Jesus, I prophesy, release, sow, plant, and cultivate in me a heart to help me lead and habitually live a blameless, honest, and just life so that all my children will be profoundly impacted and blessed.

> 10: Differing weights and differing measures—the LORD detests them both.

Suggested prayer: In the name of Jesus, I prophesy, declare, and release God's justice in all the commercial facilities in my city, so that all dishonesty against customers may dry up and die. May God's will be done in those facilities.

12: Ears that hear and eyes that see—the LORD has made them both.

Suggested prayer for you: In the name of Jesus, I prophesy, release, sow, plant, and cultivate in me ears to hear God's voice and eyes to behold his glory.

Suggested prayer for your children: In the name of Jesus, I prophesy, release, sow, plant, and cultivate in my sons and daughters [specify their names] ears to hear God's voice and eyes to behold his glory.

Suggested prayer for other people: In the name of Jesus, I prophesy, release, sow, plant, and cultivate in [specify his or her name] ears to hear God's voice and eyes to behold his glory.

Suggested prayer for national and international authorities: In the name of Jesus, I prophesy, release, sow, plant, and cultivate in [specify his or her name] ears to hear God's voice and eyes to behold his glory.

15: Gold there is, and rubies in abundance, but lips that speak knowledge are a rare jewel.

Suggested prayer for you: In the name of Jesus, I prophesy, release, sow, plant, and cultivate in me the rare jewel of lips that express knowledge, prudence, and discretion of God, lips that know how to speak.

Suggested prayer for your children: In the name of Jesus, I prophesy, release, sow, plant, and cultivate in my sons and daughters [specify their

names] the rare jewel of lips that express knowledge, prudence, and discretion of God, lips that know how to speak.

Suggested prayer for other people: In the name of Jesus, I prophesy, release, sow, plant, and cultivate in [specify his or her name] the rare jewel of lips that express knowledge, prudence, and discretion of God, lips that know how to speak.

> 18: Make plans by seeking advice; if you wage war, obtain guidance.

Suggested prayer for you: Lord Jesus, I give full opportunities and free rein for you to visit me with your advice and guidance and bring to me good advisers, so that I may make plans to win fights and battles.

Suggested prayer for your children: Lord Jesus, I give full opportunities and free rein for you to visit my sons and daughters [specify their names] with your advice and guidance and bring to them good advisers, so that they may make plans to win fights and battles.

Suggested prayer for other people: Lord Jesus, I give full opportunities and free rein for you to visit [specify his or her name] with your advice and guidance and bring to him or her good advisers, so that he or she may make plans to win fights and battles.

Suggested prayer for national and international authorities: Lord Jesus, I give full opportunities and free rein for you to visit [specify his or her name] with your advice and guidance and bring to him or her good advisers, so that he or she may make plans to win fights and battles.

> 19: A gossip betrays a confidence; so avoid a man who talks too much.

Suggested prayer for you: In the name of Jesus, I prophesy, release, sow, plant, and cultivate in me a watchful heart to help me avoid those who talk too much and help me keep aloof from gossipers and flatterers.

Suggested prayer for your children: In the name of Jesus, I prophesy, release, sow, plant, and cultivate in my sons and daughters [specify their names] watchful hearts to help them avoid those who talk too much and help them keep aloof from gossipers and flatterers.

Suggested prayer for other people: In the name of Jesus, I prophesy, release, sow, plant, and cultivate in [specify his or her name] a watchful heart to help him or her avoid those who talk too much and help him or her keep aloof from gossipers and flatterers.

> 22: Do not say, "I'll pay you back for this wrong!" Wait for the LORD, and he will deliver you.

Do not take revenge. Place before Jesus all the situations in which individuals have harmed and abused you.

Suggested prayer: In the name of Jesus, I prophesy, release, sow, plant, and cultivate in me a heart not to take revenge. Lord Jesus, I deliver and place into your hands all situations of injustice and wickedness [specify them] against me, so that the Lord may act, decide, and intervene mightily in those situations. I give full opportunities and free rein for you to save, free, and rescue me and give me a great deliverance. I declare you are my Defender, and I give you full opportunities to take care of those situations. May God's will be done in those situations.

Suggested prayer for other people: In the name of Jesus, I prophesy, release, sow, plant, and cultivate in [specify his or her name] a heart not to take revenge. Lord Jesus, I deliver and place into your hands all situations of injustice and wickedness [specify them] against him or her, so that the Lord may act, decide, and intervene mightily in those situations. May God's will be done in those situations.

24: A man's steps are directed by the LORD. How then can anyone understand his own way?

Suggested prayer for you: Lord Jesus, I give full opportunities and free rein for you to guide and determine my steps and establish your direction for what I should do and make me able to discern the way I should go.

Suggested prayer for your children: Lord Jesus, I give full opportunities and free rein for you to guide and determine the steps of my sons and daughters [specify their names] and establish their direction for what they should do and make them able to discern the way they should go.

Suggested prayer for other people: Lord Jesus, I give full opportunities and free rein for you to guide and determine the steps of [specify his or her name] and establish his or her direction for what he or she should do and make him or her able to discern the way he or she should go.

Suggested prayer for national and international authorities: Lord Jesus, I give full opportunities and free rein for you to guide and determine the steps of [specify his or her name] and establish his or her direction for what he or she should do and make him or her able to discern the way he or she should go.

28: Love and faithfulness keep a king safe; through love his throne is made secure.

Suggested prayer: In the name of Jesus, I prophesy, release, sow, plant, and cultivate in the president of my nation God's love and faithfulness. May his heart be directed by God's love. May this love make his government strong.

30: Blows and wounds cleanse away evil, and beatings
purge the inmost being.

God says severe discipline eliminates evil. We can prophesy and release what God wants.

Suggested prayer: In the name of Jesus, I prophesy and declare: may all the sorcerers and other evil individuals in my city, on TV, and in the government of my country be visited with severe beatings and with painful experiences, so that they may change and abandon their evil ways. I prophesy and release to them blows and very strong punishments to heal them from all wickedness and help transform their character. May that discipline purify their hearts profoundly. May God's will be done in their lives.

1: The king's heart is in the hand of the LORD; he directs it like a watercourse wherever he pleases.

Today those who rule the nations are the presidents. God shows he can control presidents' hearts and guide them where he wants to. God wants his righteousness in everyone, including presidents. Besides, he wants us to pray for the authorities (see 1 Timothy 2:1–4). We can, through that prophetic prayer, place presidents, governors, mayors, ministers, etc., in God's hands.

Suggested prayer: In the name of Jesus, I deliver and I place the heart of the president of my country into the hands of God. I put it under the control of the Lord Jesus, so that he may act and intervene mightily, guiding his or her thoughts toward God's justice. I give full opportunities and free rein for the Lord to determine the direction and the course of the heart of the president of my country. May his or her thoughts be guided toward the salvation, deliverance, and justice of the Lord Jesus. May his or her heart be guided to know and live God's Word. May God's will be done in the heart of the president of my country.

2: All a man's ways seem right to him, but the LORD weighs the heart.

Does someone in your family (a son, for instance) think everything he does is right and is not able to see reality? Prophesy!

Suggested prayer: Lord Jesus, I deliver and I place into your hands [add the person's name] in his or her attitude of seeing all his or her ways as pure and in his or her attitude of thinking everything he or she does is right. I give full opportunities and free rein for the Lord to judge, weigh, evaluate, adjust, correct, regulate, and guide in the right way his or her reasons and intentions.

> 5: The plans of the diligent lead to profit as surely as haste leads to poverty.

Suggested prayer for you: In the name of Jesus, I prophesy, release, sow, plant, and cultivate in me a diligent heart to make well-elaborated plans and to not get in a hurry or act too quickly.

Suggested prayer for your children: In the name of Jesus, I prophesy, release, sow, plant, and cultivate in my sons and daughters [specify their names] diligent hearts to make well-elaborated plans and to not get in a hurry or act too quickly.

Suggested prayer for other people: In the name of Jesus, I prophesy, release, sow, plant, and cultivate in [specify his or her name] a diligent heart to make well-elaborated plans and to not get in a hurry or act too quickly.

Suggested prayer for national and international authorities: In the name of Jesus, I prophesy, release, sow, plant, and cultivate in [specify his or her name] a diligent heart to make well-elaborated plans and to not get in a hurry or act too quickly.

> 11a: When a mocker is punished, the simple gain wisdom.

We do not need to give freedom for the arrogant wicked to continue in their disrespectful and mocking attitudes, shamelessly defending wickedness, adultery, homosexuality, abortion, etc. Prophesy! Agree with God, because he knows the kind of punishment mockers need.

Just prophesy. When mocking, proud individuals receive punishment for their sins, the inexperienced learn a lesson. If they are not punished, the inexperienced will imitate their mockery. God doesn't want that. What about you?

Suggested prayer: In the name of Jesus, I prophesy and declare: may all the mocking, proud individuals, witches, and sorcerers in my city, on TV, and in the government of my country be punished. I deliver and place them into the just hands of the Lord of the Armies, so that they may be disciplined as the Lord has determined in his Word. May God's will be done in their lives.

> 20a: In the house of the wise are stores of choice food
> and oil.

Another translation says: "Costly treasure and wealth are in the home of a wise person" (GW). God wants prosperity and wealth for those who are wise.

Suggested prayer: In the name of Jesus, I prophesy, release, sow, plant, and cultivate valuable treasures and wealth in the house of all the wise persons of God in my city, on TV, and in the government of my country.

> 22: A wise man attacks the city of the mighty and pulls
> down the stronghold in which they trust.

God wants us to be wise and to conquer! If you are an intercessor and spiritual warrior, you know that passage is spiritual (see Matthew 12:29 and 2 Corinthians 10:4).

Suggested prayer for you: In the name of Jesus, I prophesy, release, sow, plant, and cultivate in me a wise heart to attack and conquer the city of the mighty and pull down and demolish their defenses. I also bless all the wise persons of God in my city so they may conquer the city of the mighty and pull down and destroy their defenses.

Suggested prayer for your children: In the name of Jesus, I prophesy, release, sow, plant, and cultivate in my sons and daughters [specify their names] wise hearts to attack and conquer the city of the mighty and pull down and demolish their defenses.

Suggested prayer for other people: In the name of Jesus, I prophesy, release, sow, plant, and cultivate in [specify his or her name] a wise heart to attack and conquer the city of the mighty and pull down and demolish their defenses.

> 23: He who guards his mouth and his tongue keeps himself from calamity.

If you used to talk too much, it is time for you to protect yourself from that source of suffering. Speak very little, and when you do, speak about the gospel and the love and power of the Lord Jesus.

Suggested prayer for you: In the name of Jesus, I prophesy, release, sow, plant, and cultivate in me a wise heart to keep my mouth and tongue and take much care with what I say.

Suggested prayer for your children: In the name of Jesus, I prophesy, release, sow, plant, and cultivate in my sons and daughters [specify their names] wise hearts to keep their mouths and tongues and take much care with what they say.

Suggested prayer for other people: In the name of Jesus, I prophesy, release, sow, plant, and cultivate in [specify his or her name] a wise heart to keep his or her mouth and tongue and take much care with what he or she says.

28a: A false witness will perish.

God doesn't want the lying witness to go without punishment (see 19:5). We should agree with him.

Suggested prayer: In the name of Jesus, I prophesy and declare: may all the false witnesses in my city, on TV, and in the government of my country not go without punishment. I deliver and place them into the just hands of the Lord of the Armies, so that they may be disciplined as the Lord has determined in his Word. May God's will be done in their lives.

29b: an upright man gives thought to his ways.

Suggested prayer for you: In the name of Jesus, I prophesy, release, sow, plant, and cultivate in me an upright and wise heart to think well before giving a step and think carefully about what I should do.

Suggested prayer for your children: In the name of Jesus, I prophesy, release, sow, plant, and cultivate in my sons and daughters [specify their names] upright and wise hearts to think well before giving a step and think carefully about what they should do.

Suggested prayer for other people: In the name of Jesus, I prophesy, release, sow, plant, and cultivate in [specify his or her name] an upright and wise heart to think well before giving a step and think carefully about what he or she should do.

30: There is no wisdom, no insight, no plan that can succeed against the LORD.

If you really have in your life a project of God that is suffering opposition and misunderstanding, then this is the reality: God doesn't want anything to rise up against his project in your life!

Suggested prayer: In the name of Jesus, I prophesy and declare that no kind of wisdom, discernment, or plan will be able to oppose the Lord and his projects and purposes in my life. Lord Jesus, I give full opportunities and free rein for you to make your purpose for me prevail. I give full opportunities and free rein for the Lord to accomplish what the Lord has decided and determined for me. In the name of Jesus, I don't allow any of my plans, decisions, or ideas to be in opposition to God's project for me. May God's project for me to prevail, in the name of Jesus! May God's will for me be done, in the name of Jesus!

31b: victory rests with the LORD.

The best way to get ready for the battles we face is to recognize the victory belongs to Jesus. Begin the day by prophesying.

Suggested prayer: In the name of Jesus, in my battle [specify it] I give full opportunities and free rein for the Lord to give me power to win and conquer. I give full opportunities and free rein for the Lord to give me his victory and to help, rescue, and sustain me.

3a: A prudent man sees danger and takes refuge.

Suggested prayer for you: In the name of Jesus, I prophesy, release, sow, plant, and cultivate in me a prudent and wise heart to perceive danger and take refuge in the Lord.

Suggested prayer for your children: In the name of Jesus, I prophesy, release, sow, plant, and cultivate in my sons and daughters [specify their names] prudent and wise hearts to perceive danger and take refuge in the Lord.

Suggested prayer for other people: In the name of Jesus, I prophesy, release, sow, plant, and cultivate in [specify his or her name] a prudent and wise heart to perceive danger and take refuge in the Lord.

4: Humility and the fear of the LORD bring wealth and honor and life.

Suggested prayer for you: In the name of Jesus, I prophesy, release, sow, plant, and cultivate in me humility, gentleness, and the fear of the Lord.

Suggested prayer for your children: In the name of Jesus, I prophesy, release, sow, plant, and cultivate in my sons and daughters [specify their names] humility, gentleness, and the fear of the Lord.

Suggested prayer for other people: In the name of Jesus, I prophesy, release, sow, plant, and cultivate in [specify his or her name] humility, gentleness, and the fear of the Lord.

5a: In the paths of the wicked lie thorns and snares.

Since God's Word describes how the course of the wicked should face hindrances in their perverted ways, it is completely fair for us to agree. Would anybody like, for instance, to see a rapist with a free way to harm children and women? Let us pray for God's mercy on him to reach Jesus, but let us also prophesy so that his perverted way may be totally obstructed. You can specify the kinds of perverts who threaten the area where you live: kidnappers, murderers, thieves, etc.

Suggested prayer: In the name of Jesus, I prophesy and declare: may the way of all the sorcerers and perverts in my city, on TV, and in the government of my country be totally obstructed by thorns and traps. May God's will be done in those situations.

6: Train a child in the way he should go, and when he is old he will not turn from it.

If you are a parent, or if you intend to get married, take advantage of that orientation. We can also pray like this for other parents, so that they may know how to train their children.

Suggested prayer for you: In the name of Jesus, I prophesy, release, sow, plant, and cultivate in me a heart full of the wisdom of God's Word and open to the direction of the Holy Spirit, for me to instruct, train, and teach my children in the way in which they should walk and how they should live and behave correctly. Lord Jesus, I give full opportunities and free rein for you to make me able to train my children the right way in the right direction of their responsibilities in their lives before you. I give full opportunities and free rein for you to make me able to shoot them, as well-aimed arrows, in your life aims and ministry for them. I prophesy, declare, and determine: may they never stray from God's project for them. May God's will be done in their lives.

Suggested prayer for other people: In the name of Jesus, I prophesy, release, sow, plant, and cultivate in [specify his or her name] a heart full of the wisdom of God's Word and open to the direction of the Holy Spirit, for him or her to instruct, train, and teach his or her children in the way in which they should walk and how they should live and behave correctly. Lord Jesus, I bless him or her to give full opportunities and free rein for you to make him or her able to train his or her children the right way in the right direction of their responsibilities in their lives before you. I bless him or her to give full opportunities and free rein for you to make him or her able to shoot them, as well-aimed arrows, in your life aims and ministry for them.

> 8: He who sows wickedness reaps trouble, and the rod of his fury will be destroyed.

We do not need to give freedom for the sorcerers and other arrogant, wicked people to continue in their attitudes of shamelessly promoting wickedness, adultery, homosexuality, abortion, etc. Prophesy! Agree with God, because he knows the kind of punishment those individuals need. If every time the wicked sow perversions, they feel embarrassment and depression, will they have strength to continue advocating sin? Of course not! Without a doubt, you should pray for God's mercy on them. If they accept Jesus or not, make sure, through prayer, that they will not have any freedom to promote perversions.

Suggested prayer: In the name of Jesus, I prophesy and declare: may all the sorcerers and other arrogant wicked in my city, on TV, and in the government of my country experience affliction, disappointments, and embarrassment as they defend, praise, or teach perversions. I deliver and place them into the just hands of God, so that their pride, evil actions, and witchcraft receive all the punishments the Lord has determined in his Word. May God's will be done in those situations.

> 9: A generous man will himself be blessed, for he shares his food with the poor.

We need to prophesy blessings on generous people. That is God's will.

Suggested prayer: In the name of Jesus, I prophesy and release many blessings on all the generous men and women in my city.

If you know someone generous, make a specific prayer:

Suggested prayer: In the name of Jesus, I prophesy and release many blessings on [specify his or her name].

> 11: He who loves a pure heart and whose speech is gracious will have the king for his friend.

Do you know a sincere child of God who knows how to express with elegance and grace the wisdom and the power of God's Word? Bless him or her so that he or she may receive opportunities to be a blessing for governors and even presidents!

Suggested prayer: Lord Jesus, I deliver and place [add his or her name] into your hands, so that the Lord may act and intervene mightily in his or her life, for him or her to receive from the Lord opportunities to be a friend and counselor of important authorities. I give full opportunities and free rein for the Lord to place him or her in a position of friendship with the rulers of the country, even the president. May God's will be done in his or her life.

12: The eyes of the LORD keep watch over knowledge,
but he frustrates the words of the unfaithful.

Have you already seen how often in a TV interview someone will mock God's people and praise an individual who defends gay behavior or other perversions? We must intervene prophetically.

Suggested prayer: Lord Jesus, I give full opportunities and free rein for you to defend the truth and protect the people of good sense who teach what is good and right in my city, on TV, and in the government of my country. May the Lord overturn, frustrate, and thwart the words, the acts, and the plans of all the liars, treacherous people, sorcerers and deceivers in my city, on TV, and in the government of my country. May God's will be done in those situations.

15: Folly is bound up in the heart of a child, but the rod
of discipline will drive it far from him.

If you are a parent, you have a great responsibility toward your children, and God teaches you how to carry out that responsibility. God's Word shows *all children are already born firmly attached to foolishness*. Get spiritually ready to deliver them from that evil.

Suggested prayer: In the name of Jesus, I prophesy, release, sow, plant, and cultivate in me a wise heart to apply the rod of discipline to drive all foolishness from my children. I prophesy, release, sow, plant, and cultivate in me the wisdom of God's Word, and I open myself up to the direction and love of the Holy Spirit for me to use the rod of discipline to deliver my children from all foolishness.

Suggested prayer for other parents: In the name of Jesus, I prophesy, release, sow, plant, and cultivate in [specify his or her name] a wise heart to apply the rod of discipline to drive all foolishness from his or her children. I prophesy, release, sow, plant, and cultivate in him or her the wisdom of God's Word. I bless him or her to open himself or herself up to the direction and love of the Holy Spirit for him or her to use the rod of discipline to deliver his or her children from all foolishness.

You can also bless the rod of discipline.

Suggested prayer: In the name of Jesus, I consecrate and bless this rod to discipline, correct, teach, instruct, and deliver my children from all foolishness.

> 29: Do you see a man skilled in his work? He will serve before kings; he will not serve before obscure men.

Do you know a sincere child of God who has much competence, efficiency, and ability in his or her work? Bless this person so that he or she may experience opportunities to be promoted and be a blessing for governors and even the president!

Suggested prayer: Lord Jesus, I deliver and place [add his or her name] into your hands, so that the Lord may act and intervene mightily in his or her life, so that he or she may receive from the Lord opportunities of promotion to work in government's high functions. I give full opportunities and free rein for the Lord to place him or her in a position to work with the rulers of the country, even the president.

DAY 23

10–11: Do not move an ancient boundary stone or
encroach on the fields of the fatherless, for their Defender
is strong; he will take up their case against you.

Suggested prayer: Lord Jesus, I deliver and place into the just hands of
God all the legal situations in my city involving properties and orphans,
so that the Lord may act and intervene mightily in those situations,
defending the orphans' rights and other innocent people. Jesus, strong
and powerful God, I give you full freedom and free rein for you to act,
take care of those cases, defend the orphans' rights, and show your
justice on their behalf.

13–14: Do not withhold discipline from a child; if you
punish him with the rod, he will not die. Punish him
with the rod and save his soul from death.

This is God's message to parents and those who want to get married
someday. Sow, if you want to deliver your children from a life of
perdition. In fact, another Bible version says that by disciplining your
children you will deliver them from hell: "Thou shalt beat him with the
rod, and shalt deliver his soul from hell" (Proverbs 23:14 KJV).

Suggested prayer for you: In the name of Jesus, I prophesy, release,
sow, plant, and cultivate in me a wise heart for me not to avoid the
responsibility of applying the rod of discipline. I prophesy, release,
sow, plant, and cultivate in me the wisdom of God's Word, and I open

myself up for the direction, anointing, and love of the Holy Spirit for me to apply, without faltering and hesitation, physical discipline in my children and to deliver them from hell.

Suggested prayer for other people: In the name of Jesus, I prophesy, release, sow, plant, and cultivate in [specify his or her name] a wise heart for him or her not to avoid the responsibility of applying the rod of discipline. I prophesy, release, sow, plant, and cultivate in him or her the wisdom of God's Word, and I bless him or her to open himself or herself up for the direction, anointing, and love of the Holy Spirit for him or her to apply, without faltering and hesitation, physical discipline in his or her children and to deliver them from hell.

You can also bless the rod of discipline.

Suggested prayer: In the name of Jesus, I consecrate and bless this rod to discipline, correct, teach, instruct, and deliver my children from all foolishness and hell.

> 15–16: My son, if your heart is wise, then my heart will be glad; my inmost being will rejoice when your lips speak what is right.

You can bless your own life, your children, and other people.

Suggested prayer for you: In the name of Jesus, I prophesy, release, sow, plant, and cultivate in me a wise heart and lips to speak what is right and true.

Suggested prayer for your children: In the name of Jesus, I prophesy, release, sow, plant, and cultivate in my sons and daughters [specify their names] wise hearts and lips to speak what is right and true.

Suggested prayer for other people: In the name of Jesus, I prophesy, release, sow, plant, and cultivate in [specify his or her name] a wise heart and lips to speak what is right and true.

Suggested prayer for national and international authorities: In the name of Jesus, I prophesy, release, sow, plant, and cultivate in [specify his or her name] a wise heart and lips to speak what is right and true.

> 18: There is surely a future hope for you, and your hope will not be cut off.

When discouraged with your course in this life, release God's Word for you. Agree with what God says about you. God says you have a future and that your hope won't fail. God has rewards for you in the future.

Suggested prayer: In the name of Jesus, I declare and believe I have a good future and that my hope won't fail. Lord Jesus, I open my life completely to your rewards.

> 25: May your father and mother be glad; may she who gave you birth rejoice!

Do you want to have children who will make you glad and rejoice? Whether you are a parent or not yet, go sowing.

Suggested prayer for you: In the name of Jesus, I prophesy, release, sow, plant, and cultivate in my sons and daughters [specify their names] wise hearts to give me much joy.

Suggested prayer for other people: In the name of Jesus, I prophesy, release, sow, plant, and cultivate in the children of [specify his or her name] wise hearts to give him or her much joy.

DAY 24

3–4: By wisdom a house is built, and through understanding it is established; through knowledge its rooms are filled with rare and beautiful treasures.

If you are already married or intend to get married, get ready to build a good home.

Suggested prayer: In the name of Jesus, I prophesy, release, sow, plant, and cultivate in me and my wife (or vice versa) God's wisdom, discernment, good sense, prudence, discretion, and knowledge for us to build our home, for us to establish it and fill its rooms with all kinds of precious, excellent, beautiful, and pleasant treasures.

5–6: A wise man has great power, and a man of knowledge increases strength; for waging war you need guidance, and for victory many advisers.

Get ready for the battles that will come. If you are married, don't fail to ask for all kinds of guidance and advice from your wife. She is your best counselor.

Suggested prayer for you: In the name of Jesus, I prophesy, release, sow, plant, and cultivate in me a wise and powerful heart to have knowledge, to know how to look for orientation and right strategies to face fights and to know how to seek and accept the right advice to obtain victories.

Suggested prayer for your children: In the name of Jesus, I prophesy, release, sow, plant, and cultivate in my sons and daughters [specify their names] wise and powerful hearts to have knowledge, to know how to look for orientation and right strategies to face fights and to know how to seek and accept the right advice to obtain victories.

Suggested prayer for other people: In the name of Jesus, I prophesy, release, sow, plant, and cultivate in [specify his or her name] a wise and powerful heart to have knowledge, to know how to look for orientation and right strategies to face fights and to know how to seek and accept the right advice to obtain victories.

> 10–12: If you falter in times of trouble, how small is your strength! Rescue those being led away to death; hold back those staggering toward slaughter. If you say, "But we knew nothing about this," does not he who weighs the heart perceive it? Does not he who guards your life know it?

We should not get discouraged in this time in which so many are opposed to God's principles. Thousands of innocent children, still growing in the bellies of their mothers, are aborted, many times with the support of the law and doctors who don't respect God. Jesus calls us to help rescue those lives. "Don't fail to rescue those who are doomed to die" (Proverbs 24:11 CEV).

Suggested prayer for you: Lord Jesus, I open my life completely to your call, training, special ability, anointing, and wisdom for me to be used by you to rescue those being dragged for death, especially unborn and born children.

Suggested prayer for other people: Lord Jesus, I bless [specify his or her name] to open his or her life completely to your call, training, special ability, anointing, and wisdom for him or her to be used by you to rescue those being dragged for death, especially unborn and born children.

> 14: Know also that wisdom is sweet to your soul; if you
> find it, there is a future hope for you, and your hope
> will not be cut off.

When you are discouraged by your course in this life, release God's Word for you. Agree with what God says about you. God says you have a future and that your hope won't fail. God has rewards for you in the future.

Suggested prayer: In the name of Jesus, I declare and believe I have a good future and that my hope won't disappoint me. Lord Jesus, I open my life completely to your rewards.

> 19–20: Do not fret because of evil men or be envious
> of the wicked, for the evil man has no future hope, and
> the lamp of the wicked will be snuffed out.

Do not be sad, worried, and upset with what the wicked do, promoting adultery, homosexuality, witchcraft, etc. Prophesy!

Suggested prayer: In the name of Jesus, I prophesy and declare: may all the sorcerers and wicked in my city, on TV, and in the government of my country completely lose all direction and course in their lives of wickedness.

> 25: it will go well with those who convict the guilty, and
> rich blessing will come upon them.

We know God's opinion: he wants judges, lawyers, and other authorities to help condemn criminals!

Suggested prayer: In the name of Jesus, I deliver and place into the just hands of God all legal situations in my city, on TV, and in the government of my country. I prophesy and declare: may all the criminals be totally condemned. I deliver and place them in the just hands of God. I bless all the judges and lawyers so that they don't respect or favor the wicked and so that they help give the decision the criminals deserve! In the name of Jesus, I prophesy, declare, and release prosperity and abundant blessings on all the judges and lawyers who help in the condemnation of criminals.

> 27: Finish your outdoor work and get your fields ready;
> after that, build your house.

Before you get married, God wants you to be very established in your work and means to support a family.

Suggested prayer for you: In the name of Jesus, I prophesy, release, sow, plant, and cultivate in my life a solid commercial activity, financial stability, and means to sustain and constitute a family. Lord Jesus, I open my life completely to your special ability and power as I get ready for my business and as I prepare my business. Lord Jesus, I give you full opportunities and free rein to shepherd me and teach me to follow you and accompany you in the purpose of the construction of my home.

Suggested prayer for other people: In the name of Jesus, I prophesy, release, sow, plant, and cultivate in [specify his or her name] a solid commercial activity, financial stability, and means to sustain and constitute a family. Lord Jesus, I bless him or her to open his or her life completely to your special ability and power as he or she gets ready for his or her business and as he or she prepares his or her business. Lord Jesus, I bless him or her to give you full opportunities and free rein to shepherd him or her and teach him or her to follow you and accompany him or her in the purpose of the construction of his or her home.

29: Do not say, "I'll do to him as he has done to me; I'll pay that man back for what he did."

Suggested prayer for you: In the name of Jesus, I prophesy, release, sow, plant, and cultivate in me a patient heart not to take revenge.

Suggested prayer for other people: In the name of Jesus, I prophesy, release, sow, plant, and cultivate in [specify his or her name] a patient heart not to take revenge.

DAY 25

4–5: Remove the dross from the silver, and out comes material for the silversmith; remove the wicked from the king's presence, and his throne will be established through righteousness.

We can bless presidents, governors, and other authorities, intervening prophetically so that perverted counselors may be removed from their presence.

Suggested prayer: In the name of Jesus, I prophesy and declare: May every counselor of evil influence (who supports abortion, homosexuality, and other perversions) be removed and kept away from the presence of the president [add his or her name], governor [add his or her name], etc. May his or her government be established according to God's justice. May God's will be done in those situations.

11: A word aptly spoken is like apples of gold in settings of silver.

Is not your heart filled with joy when you say a word that brings direction, alert, advice, correction, and blessing to someone?

Suggested prayer: In the name of Jesus, I prophesy, release, sow, plant, and cultivate in me a heart and mouth that are tools of God to give right answers and advice at the right time and express my ideas well!

In the name of Jesus, I consecrate and bless my tongue to say the right word at the right time.

> 15: Through patience a ruler can be persuaded, and a gentle tongue can break a bone.

Do you want to give good advice to an authority and want your words to be heard?

Suggested prayer: In the name of Jesus, I prophesy, release, sow, plant, and cultivate in me Jesus's patience and a soft and gentle tongue. May [add the authority's name] be convinced and persuaded by the words of my lips.

> 25: Like cold water to a weary soul is good news from a distant land.

Is it not good and refreshing to receive good news from far away? If there is some hindrance, the prayer below will give room for Jesus to clear the way for the news that will cheer your heart. Be open to God's surprises.

Suggested prayer: Lord Jesus, I open my life completely to you, so that I may receive good news from far away.

3: A whip for the horse, a halter for the donkey, and a
rod for the backs of fools!

The whip is meant to direct the horse toward the right way, the halter
is to control the donkey, and the rod is to control the excesses of fools.
God knows what fools need. How could we contradict him? We need
to release that powerful word, especially when we see fools shamelessly
defending wickedness, adultery, homosexuality, abortion, etc., and still
receiving praises on TV.

Suggested prayer: In the name of Jesus, I prophesy and declare: may
the heart and mind of every fool, witch, sorcerer, pervert, and crooked
person in my city, on TV, and in the government of my country receive
discipline and correction, not praises. I prophesy, declare, and release
whip, rod, discipline, and correction for those senseless individuals'
backs, so that they may learn not to behave wickedly. I prophesy, declare,
and release God's halter to them, so that their perverted behavior may
be detained and not harm anybody. May the will of God be done in
these situations.

12: Do you see a man wise in his own eyes? There is
more hope for a fool than for him.

We need the blessing of humility.

Suggested prayer for you: In the name of Jesus, I prophesy, release, sow, plant, and cultivate in me a humble heart so that I may not see myself as a wise and intelligent person.

Suggested prayer for your children: In the name of Jesus, I prophesy, release, sow, plant, and cultivate in my sons and daughters [specify their names] humble hearts so that they may not see themselves as wise and intelligent.

Suggested prayer for other people: In the name of Jesus, I prophesy, release, sow, plant, and cultivate in [specify his or her name] a humble heart so that he or she may not see himself or herself as a wise and intelligent person.

> 17: Like one who seizes a dog by the ears is a passer-by
> who meddles in a quarrel not his own.

Suggested prayer for you: In the name of Jesus, I prophesy, release, sow, plant, and cultivate in me a prudent, wise, and patient heart so that I may not get involved in quarrels or take part in someone else's argument.

Suggested prayer for your children: In the name of Jesus, I prophesy, release, sow, plant, and cultivate in my sons and daughters [specify their names] prudent, wise, and patient hearts so that they may not get involved in quarrels or take part in someone else's argument.

Suggested prayer for other people: In the name of Jesus, I prophesy, release, sow, plant, and cultivate in [specify his or her name] a prudent, wise, and patient heart so that he or she may not get involved in quarrels or take part in someone else's argument.

DAY 27

6: Wounds from a friend can be trusted, but an enemy multiplies kisses.

Suggested prayer for you: Jesus, I give you full opportunities and free rein to bring to me and my family people who have loyalty and real friendship to us and to the Lord, for them to teach me and my family to value those loyal friends. I also give you full opportunities and free rein to keep completely away from me and my family false individuals who disguise their evil intentions.

Suggested prayer for your children: Jesus, I give you full opportunities and free rein for you to bring to my sons and daughters [specify their names] people who have loyalty and real friendship to them and to the Lord, for them to teach them to value those loyal friends. I also give you full opportunities and free rein for you to keep completely away from them false individuals who disguise their evil intentions.

12a: The prudent see danger and take refuge.

Suggested prayer for you: In the name of Jesus, I prophesy, release, sow, plant, and cultivate in me a prudent and wise heart to notice and see dangers and problems in advance, avoid them, and take refuge in the Lord.

Suggested prayer for your children: In the name of Jesus, I prophesy, release, sow, plant, and cultivate in my sons and daughters [specify their

names] prudent and wise hearts to notice and see dangers and problems in advance, avoid them, and take refuge in the Lord.

Suggested prayer for other people: In the name of Jesus, I prophesy, release, sow, plant, and cultivate in [specify his or her name] a prudent and wise heart to notice and see dangers and problems in advance, avoid them, and take refuge in the Lord.

1b: the righteous are as bold as a lion.

Jesus's righteousness in us gives us courage to face and attack evil and to promote and advance the Kingdom of God on earth.

Suggested prayer for you: In the name of Jesus, I prophesy, release, sow, plant, and cultivate in me a heart righteous, courageous, confident, and daring as a lion, which doesn't flee and isn't afraid of facing challenges.

Suggested prayer for your children: In the name of Jesus, I prophesy, release, sow, plant, and cultivate in my sons and daughters [specify their names] hearts righteous, courageous, confident, and daring as a lion, which don't flee and aren't afraid of facing challenges.

Suggested prayer for other people: In the name of Jesus, I prophesy, release, sow, plant, and cultivate in [specify his or her name] a heart righteous, courageous, confident, and daring as a lion, which doesn't flee and isn't afraid of facing challenges.

2: When a country is rebellious, it has many rulers, but a
man of understanding and knowledge maintains order.

We can sow capable men in the leadership of our country.

Suggested prayer: In the name of Jesus, I prophesy, release, sow, plant, and cultivate in the government of my country wise, intelligent, and sensible leaders who will know how to establish stability and maintain the law and order in the country, according to God's justice.

> 4: Those who forsake the law praise the wicked, but those who keep the law resist them.

Those who despise God's laws praise the wicked. Have you already seen the tendency of praising, for instance, gay "couples" who want to adopt children?

The world regards it beautiful, but such an attitude is sheer contempt against God. Let us prophesy, so that the Lord may raise up strong and intelligent men and women to oppose it and other wicked tendencies.

Suggested prayer: In the name of Jesus, I prophesy and declare: may strong and intelligent men and women be raised up in the government, media and society to fight successfully against the "new ideas and laws" from the wicked. May they be raised up to prevail and win, in the name of Jesus.

> 7a: He who keeps the law is a discerning son.

Every family wants to have wise sons and daughters who are obedient to God. Our responsibility is to pray, so that God may have, through our prayers, opportunities to act and change.

Suggested prayer: In the name of Jesus, I prophesy, release, sow, plant, and cultivate in my sons and daughters [specify their names] hearts wise and obedient to the teachings of the Word of God.

> 8: He who increases his wealth by exorbitant interest amasses it for another, who will be kind to the poor.

That is the will of God regarding exploiters' wealth. How could we disagree? See also Proverbs 13:22b.

Suggested prayer: In the name of Jesus, I prophesy and declare: may the wealth of all the exploiters in my city, on TV, and in the government of my country be transferred to the people of God who are kind to the poor.

10b: the blameless will receive a good inheritance.

We need to bless the life and witness of people who choose to avoid the evil ways.

Suggested prayer: In the name of Jesus, I bless [add his or her name] so that he or she may receive the rewards from the Lord.

Alternative suggested prayer: In the name of Jesus, I prophesy, release, sow, plant, and cultivate in [specify his or her name] a blameless heart and lips to receive the rewards from the Lord.

If you live the way God wants and are not afraid to defend truth and oppose evil, then open your life. Rewards are waiting for you!

Suggested prayer: Lord Jesus, I open my life completely to your rewards and a brilliant future.

12a: When the righteous triumph, there is great elation.

We should not have the smallest doubt: God wants the good people (according to his standard) to rule and conquer the best places in social, political, managerial, and other spheres. Let us help them, prophesying and releasing that word on them.

Suggested prayer: In the name of Jesus, I prophesy and declare: may all the righteous win and triumph in my city, state, and nation and conquer the best places in the government, so that the country may experience prosperity and peace.

14a: Blessed is the man who always fears the LORD.

A good way of understanding the fear of the Lord is to see that our love for Jesus is so strong that we fear that something may come to disturb our relationship and friendship with him. That fear is healthy and keeps us close to the Lord and away from sin. Let us cultivate that fear in us and other people.

Suggested prayer for you: In the name of Jesus, I prophesy, release, sow, plant, and cultivate in me a heart to love Jesus always and fear to turn away from his love.

Suggested prayer for your children: In the name of Jesus, I prophesy, release, sow, plant, and cultivate in my sons and daughters [specify their names] hearts to love Jesus always and fear to turn away from his love.

Suggested prayer for other people: In the name of Jesus, I prophesy, release, sow, plant, and cultivate in [specify his or her name] a heart to love Jesus always and fear to turn away from his love.

14b: he who hardens his heart falls into trouble.

What is in store for those who become hardened against the authority of God? I know the case of a TV star who alleged to love God, but she promoted eroticism. Complete heart hardness. We can bless such people, so that they may receive an "encouragement" to turn from the evil ways …

Suggested prayer: In the name of Jesus, I prophesy and declare: may the heart hardness of all the wicked on TV fall in anguishes and disappointments, so that they may abandon their evil ways and seek God.

> 16b: he who hates ill-gotten gain will enjoy a long life.

Another translation says: "One who hates dishonesty will rule a long time" (Proverbs 28:16 GNT). We need to bless the honest leaders who occupy functions in the government.

Suggested prayer: In the name of Jesus, I prophesy, release, sow, plant, and cultivate in the president, governor, mayor, judge, etc., a heart to hate dishonesty and injustice. May his or her government, through honesty, last a long time, and may he or she live many years.

An American president used to honor the homosexual movement openly. We need rulers to behave morally, not immorally.

Suggested prayer: In the name of Jesus, I prophesy, release, sow, plant, and cultivate in the government honest rulers who hate everything that is against the principles of God.

> 17: A man tormented by the guilt of murder will be a
> fugitive till death; let no one support him.

The entire society is in a panic because criminals are not only committing violence but also killing many innocent lives. Understand that if you are given an opportunity to talk personally to a murderer who is open to the Gospel, your responsibility is to speak of the love of God and show him or her that Jesus wants to save him or her from his or her sinful life. But our prayer for social well-being should generally discourage murderers. The Word of God makes it plain that they should not be free and carefree in their life of crime. If they eventually accept

Jesus, forgiveness and transformation are waiting for them. But for the overwhelming majority who don't want change, there should not be any room for them to continue their crimes in peace and without any weight in their consciences.

Suggested prayer: In the name of Jesus, I prophesy and declare: may all the murderers in my city be tormented, oppressed, and overloaded with blame for their bloodshed. May their lives of crime not receive any kind of support from corrupt lawyers. May God's will be done in their lives.

18a: He whose walk is blameless is kept safe.

We need to bless the blameless people who occupy functions in the government.

Suggested prayer: In the name of Jesus, I prophesy and declare: may all the blameless people in the government have safety and support from the Lord.

18b: he whose ways are perverse will suddenly fall.

The wicked do not need room and safety to use the laws and the government to promote homosexuality, abortion, and other wicked practices. Through prayer, we can always intervene.

Suggested prayer: In the name of Jesus, I prophesy and declare: may all the dishonest and perverted people in my city, on TV, and in the government of my country be completely weakened in their acts and words against the principles of God. May all their dishonesty and perversion fall completely and fail soon. May they have no strength to remain standing!

20a: A faithful man will be richly blessed.

Do you know people faithful to God? Then bless them!

Suggested prayer: In the name of Jesus, I prophesy and release the richest and abundant blessings of God in all people who are faithful to God in my city, on TV, and in the government of my country.

If you are faithful to God, including in tithes and offerings, then you should also be open to the blessings of God.

Suggested prayer: Lord Jesus, I open my life completely to the riches and abundant blessings from the Lord.

> 25b: he who trusts in the LORD will prosper.

Another translation says, "He who is trusting on Jehovah shall be abundantly satisfied" (Proverbs 28:25 LITV). Do you really trust in the Lord Jesus? Then open yourself to receive the blessings he has for you! He has pleasant surprises for you:

Suggested prayer: Lord Jesus, as man (or woman) who trusts in you, I open my life completely to the success, prosperity, and wealth of the Lord. Lord Jesus, I give full opportunities and free rein for you to satisfy me abundantly.

> 26: He who trusts in himself is a fool, but he who walks
> in wisdom is kept safe.

Suggested prayer for you: In the name of Jesus, I prophesy, release, sow, plant, and cultivate in me a heart not to trust in itself but to live with prudence and wisdom and escape from dangers and traps.

Suggested prayer for your children: In the name of Jesus, I prophesy, release, sow, plant, and cultivate in my sons and daughters [specify their

names] hearts not to trust in itself but to live with prudence and wisdom and escape from dangers and traps.

Suggested prayer for other people: In the name of Jesus, I prophesy, release, sow, plant, and cultivate in [specify his or her name] a heart not to trust in itself but to live with prudence and wisdom and escape from dangers and traps.

> 28: When the wicked rise to power, people go into hiding; but when the wicked perish, the righteous thrive.

We don't need to go into hiding when the wicked win an election, thinking we can do nothing. The wicked are destined for a fall if they don't change their way of life completely.

Suggested prayer: In the name of Jesus, I prophesy and declare: may all the perverts in my city and my country fall and lose all their positions in the government, and may all the righteous people multiply in the government and other positions of authority.

DAY 29

1: A man who remains stiff-necked after many rebukes
will suddenly be destroyed—without remedy.

Another translation says: "A person who will not bend after many warnings will suddenly be broken beyond repair" (Proverbs 29:1 GW). In my opinion, brokenness for a hard heart is a blessed experience. If in your family there is someone hardened, especially adult children, who doesn't want to give attention to the warnings of good sense and doesn't want to correct himself or herself, prophesy.

Suggested prayer for your children: In the name of Jesus, I prophesy and declare: may my sons and daughters [specify their names] in their heart hardness and stubbornness be completely broken. May their hard and stubborn hearts be completely broken.

Suggested prayer for other people: In the name of Jesus, I prophesy and declare: may [specify his or her name] in or her hardness and stubbornness be completely broken. May his or her hard and stubborn heart be completely broken.

2a: When the righteous thrive, the people rejoice.

When the righteous people multiply, everything gets better and everyone gets happy. Let us prophesy then for that multiplication to happen.

Suggested prayer: In the name of Jesus, I prophesy and declare: may the number of the righteous people increase and prosper in my city, on TV, and in the government of my country.

We can prophesy much more. See what another version says: "Show me a righteous ruler and I will show you a happy people" (GNT).

Suggested prayer: In the name of Jesus, I prophesy and declare: may the number of the righteous people be multiplied in positions of authority to govern my country. I prophesy, release, sow, plant, and cultivate in the government of my country many righteous people in positions of authority so that they may establish the justice of God.

> 3: A man who loves wisdom brings joy to his father, but a companion of prostitutes squanders his wealth.

Free sex has been a serious problem among young people today. Therefore, parents should sow in their children hearts to love the wisdom of God early.

Suggested prayer for your children: In the name of Jesus, I prophesy, release, sow, plant, and cultivate in my sons and daughters [specify their names] hearts to love wisdom and make their father happy.

> 4a: By justice a king gives a country stability.

We need to bless our country.

Suggested prayer: In the name of Jesus, I prophesy, release, sow, plant, and cultivate in the government of my country a righteous, wise, and honest president to govern right, exercise only the justice of God, strengthen and build the country, and give it stability. May his or her heart be filled with the justice of God.

8: Mockers stir up a city, but wise men turn away anger.

The proud wicked protest violently against the laws that limit their evil conduct. They mock and despise the principles of God, and they know how to throw a whole city into confusion and turmoil: for example, gay activists who want men to have freedom to practice their homosexual acts. But God says that the wise people will know how to act. Another version says: "Scornful men bring a city into a snare: but wise *men* turn away wrath" (KJV). A possible understanding is that wicked people's agitations for more freedom for their perversions may make a whole city open to *wrath*—that is, to tragedies and calamities. But wise men and women will know how to turn away such wrath.

They will know how to use the principles of prophetic intervention that this book teaches. Therefore, prophesy so that in your city wise people may be raised up who will know how to act prophetically against agitators and mockers who want changes in the society. We know that they are the ones who need change.

Suggested prayer: In the name of Jesus, I prophesy, release, sow, plant, and cultivate in my city, on TV, and in the government of my country wise men and women who will know how to act prophetically against the proud wicked who mock the principles of God and want to disrupt the social order. May they be raised up to turn away great social tragedies.

11: A fool gives full vent to his anger, but a wise man
keeps himself under control.

Another version says: "A fool expresses all his emotions, but a wise person controls them" (GW).

Suggested prayer for you: In the name of Jesus, I prophesy, release, sow, plant, and cultivate in me a wise, sensible, patient, and calm heart to control and restrict all my emotions.

Suggested prayer for your children: In the name of Jesus, I prophesy, release, sow, plant, and cultivate in my sons and daughters [specify their names] wise, sensible, patient, and calm hearts to control and restrict all their emotions.

Suggested prayer for other people: In the name of Jesus, I prophesy, release, sow, plant, and cultivate in [specify his or her name] a wise, sensible, patient, and calm heart to control and restrict all his or her emotions.

> 14: If a king judges the poor with fairness, his throne
> will always be secure.

A president who defends the rights of the poor (not of socialism) will govern for a long time.

Suggested prayer: In the name of Jesus, I prophesy, release, sow, plant, and cultivate in the government of my country a fair president to defend the poor with the justice of God.

> 15: The rod of correction imparts wisdom, but a child
> left to himself disgraces his mother.

A special message to mothers. Correction and discipline are a great blessing for children. Other versions say: "If they have their own way, they will make their mothers ashamed of them" (GNT). "An undisciplined child disgraces his mother" (GW).

Suggested prayer for you: In the name of Jesus, I prophesy, release, sow, plant, and cultivate in me a heart to give wisdom to my children through the discipline of the rod.

Suggested prayer for you: In the name of Jesus, I prophesy, release, sow, plant, and cultivate in me a wise heart for me not to fail in my responsibility of applying the rod of discipline. I prophesy, release, sow, plant, and cultivate in me the wisdom of the Word of God, and I open myself up to the direction, training, and love of the Holy Spirit for me to apply, without fault and hesitation, physical discipline on my children and to deliver them from hell.

Suggested prayer for your children: In the name of Jesus, I prophesy, release, sow, plant, and cultivate in my sons and daughters [specify their names] wisdom through the discipline of the rod.

Suggested prayer for other people: In the name of Jesus, I prophesy, release, sow, plant, and cultivate in [specify his or her name] a heart to give wisdom to his or her children through the discipline of the rod.

You can also bless the rod of discipline.

Suggested prayer: In the name of Jesus, I consecrate and bless this rod to discipline, correct, teach, instruct, and deliver my children from all foolishness and lack of judgement and to give them wisdom.

Now your responsibility is to use the rod the way God wants—with love and diligence.

> 17: Discipline your son, and he will give you peace; he
> will bring delight to your soul.

That subject is very important for God. The world follows a different direction and later doesn't know why so many children today suffer depression and become youth with antisocial behavior. A recent study[1] by American psychologists affirmed that every kind of physical discipline is harmful. It is their word against the Word of God. Dr. Benjamin Spock, an American psychologist pioneer in the children's

---

[1] http://www.apa.org/monitor/2012/04/spanking.aspx

rearing without any physical discipline, had a tragic experience in his personal history: his own son, who had been reared without the benefit of a rod, eventually committed suicide.

Suggested prayer for you: In the name of Jesus, I prophesy, release, sow, plant, and cultivate in me a heart to discipline, train, instruct, and correct my children with words and with the rod.

Suggested prayer for other people: In the name of Jesus, I prophesy, release, sow, plant, and cultivate in [specify his or her name] a heart to discipline, train, instruct, and correct his or her children with words and with the rod.

> 18: Where there is no revelation, the people cast off restraint; but blessed is he who keeps the law.

The revelations and visions that come from God are important for the direction of God's people. But with or without that direction, we need to be faithful in our obedience to the commandments of God. That faithfulness will bring us many blessings. That message is especially relevant for leaders.

Suggested prayer for you: In the name of Jesus, I prophesy, release, sow, plant, and cultivate in me a heart open to the prophetic orientation of the Lord through revelations and visions and open to the blessings and happiness that come through obedience to the Word of God.

Suggested prayer for your children: In the name of Jesus, I prophesy, release, sow, plant, and cultivate in my sons and daughters [specify their names] hearts open to the prophetic orientation of the Lord through revelations and visions and open to the blessings and happiness that come through obedience to the Word of God.

Suggested prayer for other people: In the name of Jesus, I prophesy, release, sow, plant, and cultivate in [specify his or her name] a heart open to the prophetic orientation of the Lord through revelations and visions and open to the blessings and happiness that come through obedience to the Word of God.

Suggested prayer for the leader of your church: In the name of Jesus, I prophesy, release, sow, plant, and cultivate in [specify his or her name] a heart open to the prophetic orientation of the Lord through revelations and visions and open to the blessings and happiness that come through obedience to the Word of God.

Suggested prayer for national and international authorities: In the name of Jesus, I prophesy, release, sow, plant, and cultivate in [specify his or her name] a heart open to the prophetic orientation of the Lord through revelations and visions and open to the blessings and happiness that come through obedience to the Word of God.

23b: a man of lowly spirit gains honor.

Suggested prayer for you: In the name of Jesus, I prophesy, release, sow, plant, and cultivate in me a gentle and humble mind and spirit.

Suggested prayer for your children: In the name of Jesus, I prophesy, release, sow, plant, and cultivate in my sons and daughters [specify their names] gentle and humble minds and spirits.

Suggested prayer for other people: In the name of Jesus, I prophesy, release, sow, plant, and cultivate in [specify his or her name] a gentle and humble mind and spirit.

26: Many seek an audience with a ruler, but it is from the LORD that man gets justice.

Are you in need of the assistance of someone important to solve a cause? There is no one stronger than the Lord Jesus. Put your life and your cause before him.

Suggested prayer for you: Lord Jesus, I deliver and place into your hands my cause [specify it], so that the Lord may act and intervene mightily in that situation. I declare you as powerful God to take care of my cause. May the will of God be done in that situation.

Suggested prayer for your children: Lord Jesus, I deliver and place into your hands the cause [specify it] of my sons and daughters [specify their names], so that the Lord may act and intervene mightily in that situation. I declare you as powerful God to take care of their cause. May the will of God be done in that situation.

Suggested prayer for other people: Lord Jesus, I deliver and place into your hands the cause [specify it] of [specify his or her name], so that the Lord may act and intervene mightily in that situation. I declare you as powerful God to take care of his or her cause. May the will of God be done in that situation.

DAY 30

5: Every word of God is flawless; he is a shield to those
who take refuge in him.

If you are going through some serious problem, know that each word of
God is a sure promise of victory for you: God fulfills every promise that
he makes. Take refuge in Jesus and he will protect and will defend you.

Suggested prayer: Lord Jesus, in the situation in which I am [specify
it], I take refuge in you and I declare you my shield, my protection, and
my safety. I declare you my Defender and my Protector, and I give full
opportunities and free rein for you to protect me and defend me. I also
give you full opportunities and free rein for you to fulfill your promises
in my life.

18–19: There are three things that are too amazing for
me, four that I do not understand: the way of an eagle in
the sky, the way of a snake on a rock, the way of a ship
on the high seas, and the way of a man with a maiden.

Another version says: "The way of the eagle in the heavens, The way of a
serpent on a rock, The way of a ship in the heart of the sea, *And the way
of a man in youth*" (verse 19 YLT, italics mine). As reality shows, human
feelings are so strong that there can be unexpected results when a young
man and a girl go out together. Unexpected situations and emotions may
arise when a man and a woman are very close. That is not a secret for
us. There may appear dangers, because although that passage may seem

obscure, if we analyze it in the context, we will see that verse 20 reveals a sinful situation involving a sexual relationship. Therefore, if you have children and want them to be led prudently toward marriage, begin to prophesy. Before the unpleasant surprises come in your children's youth, sow in them a spouse chosen and anointed by God. After Jesus, the most important relationship in a person's life is with a spouse. While your children are young, you can place your hands on their heads, one by one, to prophesy and bless them.

Suggested prayer for your sons: Lord Jesus, I give and deliver my sons [specify their names] into your hands, so that the Lord may act and intervene mightily in their sentimental and sexual lives. I give full opportunities and free rein for the Lord to accompany them in their way to inherit a prudent wife (see Proverbs 19:14). I bless and consecrate them to inherit from you wise, prudent, and intelligent wives. I prophesy, release, sow, plant, and cultivate in them wise, prudent and intelligent wives. Lord Jesus, I give full opportunities and free rein for you to go ahead of them and prosper their way to inherit their wives (see Genesis 24:7, 40).

Suggested prayer for your daughters (adapted): Lord Jesus, I give and deliver my daughters [specify their names] into your hands, so that the Lord may act and intervene mightily in their sentimental and sexual lives. I give full opportunities and free rein for the Lord to accompany them in their way to inherit prudent husbands. I bless and consecrate them to inherit from you wise, prudent, and intelligent men. I prophesy, release, sow, plant, and cultivate in them wise, prudent, and intelligent men. Lord Jesus, I give full opportunities and free rein for you to go ahead of them and prosper their way to inherit their husbands.

10–31: A wife of noble character who can find? She is worth far more than rubies. Her husband has full confidence in her and lacks nothing of value. She brings him good, not harm, all the days of her life. She selects wool and flax and works with eager hands. She is like the merchant ships, bringing her food from afar. She gets up while it is still dark; she provides food for her family and portions for her servant girls. She considers a field and buys it; out of her earnings she plants a vineyard. She sets about her work vigorously; her arms are strong for her tasks. She sees that her trading is profitable, and her lamp does not go out at night. In her hand she holds the distaff and grasps the spindle with her fingers. She opens her arms to the poor and extends her hands to the needy. When it snows, she has no fear for her household; for all of them are clothed in scarlet. She makes coverings for her bed; she is clothed in fine linen and purple. Her husband is respected at the city gate, where he takes his seat among the elders of the land. She makes linen garments and sells them, and supplies the merchants with sashes. She is clothed with strength and dignity; she can laugh at the days to come. She speaks with wisdom, and faithful instruction is on her tongue. She watches over the affairs of her household and does not eat the bread of idleness. Her children arise and call her blessed; her husband also, and he praises her: "Many women do noble things, but you surpass them all." Charm is deceptive, and beauty is fleeting; but a woman who fears the LORD is to be praised. Give her the reward she has earned, and let her works bring her praise at the city gate.

The best and greatest investment a man can make is to sow a wife of virtue and noble character in his life. The Word of God describes how an ideal wife is. We can, with such an orientation, sow. A married man can sow that ideal wife in his wife. A single man can sow such a woman in his life.

Suggested prayer for married men: In the name of Jesus, I prophesy, release, sow, plant, and cultivate in my wife [add her name] a strong exemplary, capable, virtuous character, much more valuable than rubies. I declare that I will have full trust in her, and I will never lack anything good. She will do me good and not evil all the days of her life. She will employ all her living for my good.[2] She will work gladly and will have initiative to lead a business enterprise in our home. She will bring our food from far away. She will get up before daylight to prepare food for our family and administer her tasks. She will evaluate a property and will buy it. She will plant a vineyard from the profits she is going to earn. She will work with energy; her arms will be strong and vigorous. She will administer her lucrative trade well, she will know when to buy or sell, and she will be busy until late at night. She will welcome oppressed people and will help needy people. She will have no fear for me and our children when winter comes, because all of us will dress in warm clothing. She will know how to make beautiful clothes, and she will wear them with discretion, elegance, and purity. I will be respected and known in the most important places in my city, where I will be

---

2   As Septuagint. (Proverbs 31:12 Brenton)

between the authorities and the most important people. She will be prosperous in her home business, and her products will be successful in the market.

She will dress with strength, nobility, honor, grace, excellence, elegance, and dignity. She will smile at the future, without fear. She will open her lips to speak with wisdom, and she will teach with love and will give advice with much prudence. She will always keep a close eye out and will give much attention to everything happening with me and our children, and she will always be ready to take care of our needs. She will be attentive to our children's behavior and with whom they walk. She will take care of the affairs of her home, and she won't give room to laziness. Our children will get up and will praise her; I will also praise her, saying, "Many women are an exemplary model, but you surpass all of them in excellence, kindness, virtue, and noble attitudes." May she receive the reward she deserves, and may her actions be praised in the most important places in our city. I will praise her, and I will respect her before all, because she will deserve it.

Suggested prayer for single men: In the name of Jesus, I prophesy, release, sow, plant, and cultivate in my life an exemplary, capable, virtuous wife of strong character, much more valuable than rubies. I declare that I will have full trust in her, and I will never lack anything good. She will do me good and not evil all the days of her life. She will employ all her living for my good.[3] She will work gladly and will have initiative to lead a business enterprise in our home. She will bring our food from far away. She will get up before daylight to prepare food for our family and administer her tasks. She will evaluate a property and will buy it. She will plant a vineyard from the profits she is going to earn. She will work with energy; her arms will be strong and vigorous. She will administer her lucrative trade well, she will know when to

---

3   As Septuagint. (Proverbs 31:12 Brenton)

buy or sell, and she will be busy until late at night. She will welcome oppressed people and will help needy people. She will have no fear for me and our children when winter comes, because all of us will dress in warm clothing. She will know how to make beautiful clothes, and she will wear them with discretion, elegance, and purity. I will be respected and known in the most important places in my city, where I will be between the authorities and the most important people. She will be prosperous in her home business, and her products will be successful in the market. She will dress with strength, nobility, honor, grace, excellence, elegance, and dignity. She will smile at the future without fear. She will open her lips to speak with wisdom, and she will teach with love and will give advice with much prudence. She will always keep a close eye out and will give much attention to everything happening with me and our children, and she will always be ready to take care of our needs. She will be attentive to our children's behavior and with whom they walk. She will take care of the affairs of her home, and she won't give room to laziness. Our children will get up and will praise her; I will also praise her, saying, "Many women are an exemplary model, but you surpass all of them in excellence, kindness, virtue and noble attitudes." May she receive the reward she deserves, and may her actions be praised in the most important places in our city. I will praise her, and I will respect her before all, because she will deserve it.

Suggested prayer for women: In the name of Jesus, I prophesy, release, sow, plant, and cultivate in me a strong exemplary, capable, virtuous character, much more valuable than rubies. I declare that my husband will have full trust in me, and he will never lack anything good. I will do him good and not evil all the days of my life. I will employ all my living for his good.[4] I will work gladly and will have initiative to lead a business enterprise in our home. I will bring our food from far away. I will get up before daylight to prepare food for our family and

---

4   As Septuagint. (Proverbs 31:12 Brenton)

administer my tasks. I will evaluate a property and will buy it. I will plant a vineyard from the profits I am going to earn. I will work with energy; my arms will be strong and vigorous. I will administer my lucrative trade well, I will know when to buy or sell, and I will be busy until late at night. I will welcome oppressed people and will help needy people. I will have no fear for him and our children when winter comes, because all of us will dress in warm clothing. I will know how to make beautiful clothes, and I will wear them with discretion, elegance, and purity. My husband will be respected and known in the most important places in his city, where he will be between the authorities and the most important people. I will be prosperous in my home business, and my products will be successful in the market. I will dress with strength, nobility, honor, grace, excellence, elegance, and dignity. I will smile at the future, without fear. I will open my lips to speak with wisdom, and I will teach with love and will give advice with much prudence. I will always keep a close eye out and will give much attention to everything happening with him and our children, and I will always be ready to take care of our needs. I will be attentive to our children's behavior and with whom they walk. I will take care of the affairs of my home, and I won't give room to laziness. Our children will get up and will praise me; my husband will also praise me, saying, "Many women are an exemplary model, but you surpass all of them in excellence, kindness, virtue, and noble attitudes." May I receive the reward I deserve, and may my actions be praised in the most important places in our city. My husband will praise me, and he will respect me before all, because I will deserve it.

APPENDIX

Solomon
Success, wealth, women, and follies from the wisest man

One of the gifts you most need is wisdom: "Blessed is the man who finds wisdom, the man who gains understanding, for she is more profitable than silver and yields better returns than gold. She is more precious than rubies; nothing you desire can compare with her" (Proverbs 3:13–15). The good news is the Lord wants to give that precious gift to all who need and ask with faith:

> If any of you lacks wisdom, he should ask God, who gives generously to all without finding fault, and it will be given to him. But when he asks, he must believe and not doubt, because he who doubts is like a wave of the sea, blown and tossed by the wind. (James 1:5–6)

For you to be able to use God's revelations in his Word, you need God's wisdom and let him use and guide that wisdom. It is not enough to have a spiritual gift. It is necessary to let God use it. Proverbs was written by Solomon, son of David, king of Israel (see Proverbs 1:1), a man who asked and received wisdom from God. Yet he was not able to let the Lord guide his life until the end. It is necessary to know a little of the life of Proverbs' author, so that you may learn how to give to God opportunities for him to use you and the gifts he gives you and so that you may learn how to live and apply all the wisdom of Proverbs.

Solomon's life stands out not only for his fame and wealth but also his extraordinary wisdom and the way he chose to live it. Besides Proverbs, he is also the author of the biblical books of Song of the Songs, Ecclesiastes, and Psalms 72 and 127.

Living in a time when it was common for men, especially rulers, to have more than one wife, with his wisdom Solomon was able to see a truth that nobody else seemed to be seeing: the perfect plan of God for the sexual relationship is a husband loving only one wife (see Proverbs 5:15–19). Only the wisdom that comes from the Lord could let him understand the right plan of God for marriage. With such a revelation, he was able to teach men to have a love commitment with only one woman: "Be faithful to your own wife and give your love to her alone. So be happy with your wife and find your joy with the woman you married" (Proverbs 5:15–18 GNT.) With such a revelation, he knew the key to live a victorious life as a man and as a king.

Solomon also received a special revelation showing that it is the Lord who builds the home (see Psalm 127:1), especially through a wise wife (see Proverbs 14:1). Where does such a woman come from? Solomon knew very well, because he wrote: "a prudent wife is from the Lord" (Proverbs 19:14b). He also understood how God wanted to use him, together with the wife that the Lord was going to give him, to bring up victorious children to advance the purposes of the Lord in this world. He wrote:

> Sons are a heritage from the LORD, children a reward from him. Like arrows in the hands of a warrior are sons born in one's youth. Blessed is the man whose quiver is full of them. They will not be put to shame when they contend with their enemies in the gate. (Psalm 127:3–5)

Solomon saw clearly that the project of the Lord is to give to his servants children to be trained for the special purposes of the Lord. In Proverbs, he gave many instructions on how to rear and discipline children. He was completely equipped to form a family. Everything he needed to do was to open himself for the promise of God, which he had received, that a prudent wife comes from the Lord. He only had to wait the Lord to bring such woman.

God was preparing everything for Solomon to have a special marriage. Even his mother was being used by the Lord to encourage him to follow the plan of God of having a love commitment with only one woman. She tried to direct him for a right choice of marriage. In Proverbs 31:10–31, she gave him valuable suggestions on how to choose a wise wife of virtue and character, who would help him to be an excellent king. She also advised him not to get involved with several women:

> You are my own dear son, the answer to my prayers. What shall I tell you? Don't spend all your energy on sex and all your money on women; they have destroyed kings. (Proverbs 31:2–3 GNT)

However, he was not able to follow his mother's instructions. He didn't also have patience to wait the Lord fulfill the promise of bringing him a prudent wife. Instead of using his wisdom to obey God, he let his sexual and political impulses guide his wisdom and life. To have peace with other countries, it was customary in that time for a ruler to get married to the ruler's daughter from the other country. So by making alliance with several countries, Solomon became attached to many pagan foreign women.

> Solomon loved many foreign women. Besides the daughter of the king of Egypt he married Hittite women

and women from Moab, Ammon, Edom, and Sidon. (1
Kings 11:1 GNT)

He was fully aware that he was making wrong choices of marriages: "He
married them even though the LORD had commanded the Israelites
not to intermarry with these people, because they would cause the
Israelites to give their loyalty to other gods" (1 Kings 11:2 GNT). The
Word of God contains very clear and specific instructions about our
sexual lives, and it is not necessary to look for a supernatural direction
from the Holy Spirit to discover if it is right or wrong to have many
women. Even the simplest people who read God's Word know God's
will for sexuality. Thousands of simple men and women have been able
to live a married life according God's project. It is not necessary to have
Solomon's superwisdom to obey the plainest commandments of God.

Often Solomon read in his Bible:

> The king is not to have many wives, because this would
> make him turn away from the LORD; and he is not to
> make himself rich with silver and gold. (Deuteronomy
> 17:17 GNT)

Although he knew God's will, later in his life Solomon reached the
point where he had "700 wives who were princesses and three hundred
wives who were concubines" (1 Kings 11:3 GW). He himself confessed,
"I had all the women a man could want" (Ecclesiastes 2:8b GNT). He
was able to form the largest harem in the world. Regarding silver and
gold, he said: "I amassed silver and gold for myself, and the treasure of
kings and provinces" (Ecclesiastes 2:8a).

Weakness and Wicked Women

How was Solomon able to get involved with so many heathen women? Before Solomon acquired the habit of collecting women, the people of Israel worshiped God, but according to some pagan customs:

> The people were still sacrificing at other worship sites because a temple for the name of the LORD had not yet been built. (1 Kings 3:2 GW)

Those "other worship sites" were places that had not been established by God but by pagan customs. In spite of his wisdom, Solomon was not worshiping God in a way different from the people.

> Solomon loved the LORD and lived by his father David's rules. However, he still sacrificed and burned incense at these other worship sites. (1 Kings 3:3 GW)

It is astonishing how he didn't want to let go this religious weakness so popular at that time, even though God's Word hadn't given him an example in that direction. There was the place designated by God where everyone was to sacrifice, but Solomon had the weakness of sacrificing in other places. He knew that the law of God prohibited sacrifices out of the place established by God:

> Any Israelite who sacrifices an ox, a lamb or a goat in the camp or outside of it instead of bringing it to the entrance to the Tent of Meeting to present it as an offering to the LORD in front of the tabernacle of the LORD—that man shall be considered guilty of bloodshed; he has shed blood and must be cut off from his people. (Leviticus 17:3–4)

However, he didn't want to follow the simple wisdom of God's Word that he knew so well. Even if his father David had been negligent in that area, Solomon had a wisdom that could help him to behave better and teach the people to behave better. But he chose to remain in the weakness of the popular customs, worshiping the right God in the wrong way. His wrong way to sacrifice to God may have opened a spiritual breach that facilitated his fall with heathen women.

Although in the Old Testament there was tolerance toward men who had more than one wife, the Bible shows that Solomon's sexual life went beyond all limits:

> King Solomon, however, loved many foreign women besides Pharaoh's daughter-Moabites, Ammonites, Edomites, Sidonians and Hittites. They were from nations about which the LORD had told the Israelites, "You must not intermarry with them, because they will surely turn your hearts after their gods." Nevertheless, Solomon held fast to them in love. He had seven hundred wives of royal birth and three hundred concubines, and his wives led him astray. As Solomon grew old, *his wives turned his heart after other gods,* and his heart was not fully devoted to the LORD his God, as the heart of David his father had been. *He followed* Ashtoreth the goddess of the Sidonians, and Molech the detestable god of the Ammonites. So Solomon did evil in the eyes of the LORD; he did not follow the LORD completely, as David his father had done. On a hill east of Jerusalem, *Solomon built a high place* for Chemosh the detestable god of Moab, and for Molech the detestable god of the Ammonites. *He did the same for all his foreign wives,* who burned incense and *offered sacrifices to their gods.* The LORD became angry with Solomon because his

heart had turned away from the LORD, the God of Israel, who had appeared to him twice. (1 Kings 11:1–9, *italics mine*)

The darkest point in Solomon's involvement with those women is that their idolatry was associated to satanic worship and baby sacrifices. He followed their religions, knowing very well what had happened in the past when God's people got involved with heathen women:

> They intermarried with them and adopted their pagan ways. God's people worshiped idols, and this caused their destruction. They offered their own sons and daughters as sacrifices to the idols of Canaan. They killed those innocent children, and the land was defiled by those murders. They made themselves impure by their actions and were unfaithful to God. (Psalm 106:35–39 GNT)

King David had, besides his son Solomon, many other descendants who became kings. The Bible shows the number of children those kings had. For example, King Rehoboam, the son of Solomon and the grandson of David, had in all twenty-eight sons and sixty daughters (see 2 Chronicles 11:21). God's Word also records how many children David had. However, strangely, no reference has ever been made about the number of children Solomon had with his one thousand women. What happened to all the children he begot?

No one knows. There is an almost scary silence involving this question. Yet we know that his women were pagan and that he followed their religions.

Therefore, you can have a clue on what happened to the more than one thousand sons and daughters who would have probably been recorded in the Bible if the idol worship in that time did not require baby sacrifices.

Even though perhaps he did not sacrifice his children himself, yet he built all the high places his wives needed to make their "sacrifices." He loved them so much that he was willing to do anything for them and to let them do anything.

Obsessed with the Erotic Love

The Word of God doesn't fail to reveal what was happening in his heart. One of his books shows his deepest desires and feelings. The Song of the Songs is an intensely erotic poem of Solomon, and it is dedicated to his sexual desires directed to a woman in a specific time of his life. At the time when he alleged to love Shulammite, he had *only 140 wives*, not to mention the virgin girls (see Song of Songs 6:8b GNT). Even with such a high number of women, he managed still to acquire another eight hundred.

Song of the Songs doesn't contain any mention of God, but some Bible commentators, with much good will, try to spiritualize it or even apply its eroticism to the normal marital love. But the truth is that if you could really apply its erotic message to a Christian (or secular) marriage, you would have to accept its obvious implications: since Solomon's *marital* love in the Song of the Songs includes relationships with many heathen women, does that mean that each Christian husband is also entitled to a Shulammite together with a harem of heathen women?

Therefore, from a purely realistic viewpoint, Song of the Songs does not express a normal marital love but just the intensely erotic life of Solomon. When he wrote that book, he had some two hundred women. And he was only beginning to invest in his harem! With that number of women, Solomon no longer understood what marital love was. He didn't have a normal marital life; he had only a deep and exotic sexual life. The center of his attention was merely sex.

One Thousand Songs for One Thousand Women

What did Solomon feel for Shulammite? Love. How many women did he eventually have? One thousand. What did he feel for them? Love. To Shulammite, he wrote an erotic poem, also considered a song. But the Bible shows that he wrote about one thousand songs … If those songs really had a content of spiritual edification (as the book of Proverbs), it is safe to presume that you would have access today to each one of those songs. There is the collection of songs of David, his father, incorporated in the book of Psalms. You would have a book of Psalms that is larger or another collection of songs with another title. And that collection should be very special, because Solomon had been blessed with a wisdom that his father didn't have.

Probably even David, in his heart, had hope that Solomon, with all his intelligence, could bless the people of God with a literary and musical legacy much wider than David himself had done. Solomon had the wisdom to write and compose, but he didn't possess the dedication to God that his father had. His attention and love were deeply entertained by the beauty and pleasures of his many wives. "Solomon was obsessed with their love" (1 Kings 11:2b GW).

Perhaps, as every womanizer, Solomon had the habit of composing erotic poems for each woman that he acquired. If he, in his love, wrote a song for Shulammite, why would he forget his other one thousand wives? Since there is biblical evidence that he loved them, who could suggest that he didn't also compose songs for them?

The Bible says that Solomon "composed three thousand proverbs and more than a thousand songs" (1 Kings 4:32 GNT). The word *song* used here in the original Hebrew (*shiyr*) it is the same word used in Song of the Songs 1:1.

However, all the songs were lost, except the Song of the Songs, which may be considered a sample of what he used to compose.

Sex and Money

Of the one thousand songs Solomon composed, God might have preserved Song of the Songs in order to show that even the wisest man of God, if he doesn't keep himself attached to God in the sexual area, can suffer serious spiritual weakness and defeat (see 1 Kings 11:1–8).

The two primary reasons for great men's fall are women and money. In the case of Solomon, if some Bible commentator tried to explain that he fell because of sex, he would not be writing about any new idea. The Word of God itself has already given that explanation:

> Was it not because of marriages like these that Solomon king of Israel sinned? Among the many nations there was no king like him. He was loved by his God, and God made him king over all Israel, but even he was led into sin by foreign women. (Nehemiah 13:26)

Regarding money, it is possible to notice that Solomon didn't follow the example of David his father. While David gave extremely generous gifts to God (see 1 Chronicles 22:14; 29:2–5), all that we know it is that Salomon accumulated riches. While David amassed for God, Solomon amassed for himself (see Ecclesiastes 2:8a).

Differences between David and Solomon

David didn't have as much wisdom as Solomon did, but even so he acted with much prudence, according the "little" wisdom he had. "In everything he did he had great success, because the LORD was with him" (1 Samuel 18:14). The Septuagint explains better the reason David had so much success in everything he did: "And David was prudent in all his ways, and the Lord was with him" (1 Samuel 18:14 Brenton). He was not perfect, but he was a man who always sought to behave with discretion and modesty.

Like his son Solomon, David also felt strong sexual desires. He had an intense marital life. But the difference between David and Solomon was the difference between modesty and immodesty. While David kept his sexual intimacy a strictly personal marital subject, Solomon did not.

The sexual intimacy that David kept, Solomon exposed. The wisdom that Solomon had did come from God, but when his heart turned from the Lord and became firmly attached to a crowd of pagan women, he started to be directed by his own carnal impulses, and his wisdom started to serve those urges. What is the difference between a carnal wisdom and a wisdom from God in a man who no longer opens himself up to God? Little. The same satisfaction that Solomon had in exposing his sexual intimacy through erotic songs is very evident in carnal individuals in the world who have pleasure in revealing on TV, through microphones, and in any other way their nakedness and sexual appetites.

> Every prudent man acts out of knowledge, but a fool
> exposes his folly. (Proverbs 13:16)

A man who has good sense behaves with discretion and modesty in order to avoid what is inappropriate and inconvenient. Song of the Songs is a contrast of the discreet behavior that is part of a man or woman who respects himself/herself as a temple of the Holy Spirit, especially in the most intimate area. First Corinthians 12:23, in three different Bible versions, shows, in a beautiful example, how the body of Christ, which is us, values itself and behaves:

And the parts that we think are less honorable we treat with special honor. And the parts that are unpresentable are treated with special modesty.

We take special care to dress up some parts of our bodies. We are modest about our personal parts. (CEV)

Those parts of the body which we think to be less honorable, on those we bestow more abundant honor; and our unpresentable parts have more abundant propriety. (WEB)

Another difference between David and his son Solomon: David sinned sexually once, but he repented and never returned to that sin. In contrast, Solomon began getting involved sexually with many women, in disobedience to God, and remained for the rest of his life in that sin.

Some kings descending from David, like Jehoshaphat, Hezekiah, and Josiah, even not possessing Solomon's wisdom, made an effort to imitate the life of prudence of David. Solomon could have left an example of life of much more prudence, but in his sensuality he wasted the intelligence God gave him.

We know that there was in David a very big passion, because he wrote much on what he felt. Many Psalms express the feelings of the soul of David before God. We also know that there was in Solomon an equally big passion … But the difference between them was enormous. While the supreme passion of David was directed toward God, the passion of Solomon was directed toward countless heathen women.

However, who could blame Solomon for not loving God as much as his father David did? With so many women, who would be able to have time to think of God? Even if he had only 140 women, his agenda would have been full with other commitments, including the spiritual ones, for the rest of his life. Certainly, he also didn't have much time for each wife.

Important Phases of the Wisest Man's Life

We can divide Solomon's life in three parts: before (when he wrote and lived Proverbs), during (when he wrote and lived Song of the Songs), and later (when he wrote and lived Ecclesiastes).

In Proverbs, we see a Solomon who felt pleasure in obeying God. Proverbs shows very well his wisdom, in his years of obedience, when God was his main pleasure. He became the wisest man in the world!

In Song of the Songs, we see a Solomon submersing in his sexual pleasures. Song of the Songs shows very well his eroticism, in the period when he was forming the largest harem in the world and having sex with an enormous crowd of beautiful pagan women, in direct disobedience to the commandments of God. He became the greatest womanizer in the world!

In Ecclesiastes, we see a Solomon already old and deeply tired of all pleasures. Ecclesiastes shows very well his complete dissatisfaction with the pleasures and joys of life, an inevitable result of a life turned away from God. He got tired of amassing wealth and women. He became the most unhappy man in the world!

Of the women he had, was Shulammite really his favorite? It is not what he says: "I do know there is one good man in a thousand, but never have I found a good woman" (Ecclesiastes 7:28b CEV). He was speaking through experience. In the end of his life, having loved one thousand women, he admitted that he didn't find any one among them who really pleased him! The pleasure abundance left him discontented with everything, including his own life and his crowd of wives.

However, if he had let the Lord visit him in his sexual and sentimental area, would not Solomon have received the blessing of finding a good and ideal wife? (See Proverbs 18:22.) Certainly, God had a right choice for him, but he preferred to make one thousand wrong choices! He was a man who was blessed with the wonderful revelation of the excellent wife of Proverbs 31, but he was not able to open himself to receive from the Lord such a woman. He spent the best years of his life occupied in the privacy of his harem, doing exactly what his mother had tried to dissuade him from: spending all his energy on sex (see Proverbs 31:3 GNT).

Ecclesiastes shows Solomon ended his life as a wise old man with a heart that still knew how to recognize the reality of God but was no longer able to feel him and experience him. While many Psalms reveal David feeling and experiencing the presence of God, Ecclesiastes shows Solomon living the emptiness of that presence. He ended unsatisfied and empty of the Holy Spirit's joys because he chose not to let God guide and use his wisdom. Then why didn't he lose his gift of wisdom? Because "God doesn't take back the gifts he has given" (Romans 11:29 CEV).

If Solomon had lived until the end of his life according to the wisdom he taught in Proverbs, he would have been the happiest man in the world: he would have married a woman of virtue and character (see Proverbs 31:10-31), who would have encouraged him in his walk with God and would have given him wise advice to help him rule well. He would have been faithful to her and given his love only to her (see Proverbs 5:15 GNT), and she would have loved him and always made him happy (see Proverbs 5:19b GNT). He would have had wise and special children (see Psalm 127:3–5), who would have brought him much joy (see Proverbs 10:1a) and would have combatted in the wars of the Lord. Besides, he would have learned by experience that a wise and prudent wife who comes from the Lord (see Proverbs 19:14) is a blessing worth far more than rubies and a harem of one thousand women. For that and other reasons, he would have always felt joy and pleasure in his God and in his own life.

The happiness that Solomon refused, you can reach. He died without applying and living many of the wonderful promises he wrote of in Proverbs and in Psalm 127. However, you can experience them, by cultivating the ability to deeply respect the Lord Jesus and his powerful Word: "The fear of the LORD *is* the beginning of wisdom" (Proverbs 9:10a KJV). The only kind of wisdom that really brings blessings and happiness is to love and respect God above all.